PARENTS' COLLEGE SURVIVAL GUIDE:

PLANNING AND PAYING FOR COLLEGE

by John S. Groleau, CCPS, MSFS

PARENTS' COLLEGE SURVIVAL GUIDE:
PLANNING AND PAYING FOR COLLEGE

by John S. Groleau, CCPS, MSFS
with Layla Groleau

ISBN 978-0983605508

Lighthouse Financial Publishing
as a division of Lighthouse Financial Group, Inc.

John S. Groleau, CCPS, MSFS
Lighthouse Financial Group, Inc.
66 Miller Drive, Suite. 104
North Aurora, IL 60542
(630) 907-9830 * (630) 907-9831 Fax

Dedication

To Vincent P. Mainelli 1935-2010

My first mentor... you had the patience
of Job and the love of a father

You are missed.

Acknowledgements

I would like to acknowledge the following for their invaluable assistance in this project:

The family and staff at Lighthouse College Planning, the hundreds of families who have given me the singular honor to help them achieve their dreams, Peg Hendershot at Career Vision for recommending that I become a financial planner, Scott Moffitt who has been a good friend and colleague, Eileen Stephens, "coach" Joe Lukacs, Shilanski and Associates for teaching me how to run a business, Landmark Education for helping me create the possibility, the Letts family for starting me on the college journey, my children who have been such an inspiration for me to grow as a father and as a professional, my mother, JoAnne, who helped me to believe that I could accomplish anything in life if I wanted it badly enough, and my wife Layla, my "Hard headed woman" for always believing in me even when I didn't.

TABLE OF CONTENTS

Chapter 4: Getting a Smart Start.......... 39
LESSONS FROM THE TITANIC

Chapter 5 45
"IT AIN'T EASY BEING GREEN"

Chapter 6: Marketability Mistakes....... 57
MADISON AVENUE GOES TO COLLEGE

Chapter 7: Degrees Offered by Various Colleges Help Narrow the Search........ 65
"WHAT ARE YOU LOOKIN' AT?" by Layla

Chapter 11: Applications and Essays ...103
"STRUTTIN' YOUR STUFF" by Shireen

Chapter 12: The EFC or.....................121
EXTREMELY SCREWED-UP CALCULATION

Chapter 18: Parent and Student Case Studies 169
"THE GOOD, THE BAD..."

Chapter 19: Cash Flow, Debt, etc.........181
"... AND THE UGLY"

INTRODUCTION

In a powerful 60 Minutes television segment a number of insights were revealed on today's generation of sixteen- to twenty-year-olds, which is the largest generation of young people since the '60s. The segment, called "Echo Boomers," explained that these children now coming of age are called "echo boomers" because they're the genetic offspring and demographic echo of their parents, the baby boomers. Born between 1982 and 1995, there are nearly 80 million of them, and they're already having a huge impact on entire segments of the economy. As our population ages, they will be become the next dominant generation of Americans.

The segment went on to point out that "echo boomers are a reflection of the dramatic changes in American life over the past 20 years. They are the first to grow up with computers at home, in a 500-channel TV universe. They are multi-taskers with cell phones, music downloads, and Instant Messaging on the Internet. They are totally plugged-in citizens of a worldwide community."

"This is a generation that aims to please—their parents, friends, teachers and college admissions officers. It's a generation in which rules seem to have replaced rebellion, convention is winning out over individualism, and values are very traditional."

They are also the most diverse generation ever — 35 percent are non-white — and the most tolerant, believing everyone should be part of the community.

Historian Neil Howe, along with co-author William Strauss, has made a career studying different generations. Howe has stated, 'All the research on echo boomers always reflects the same thing: They are much different than their self-absorbed, egocentric baby boomer parents. Nothing could be more anti-boom than being a good team player, right? Fitting in. Worrying less about leadership than follower-ship. If you go into a public school today, teamwork is stressed everywhere. Team teaching, team grading, collaborative sports, community service, service learning, student juries, the list goes on and on.'

Howe believes Boomers are more like their grandparents, the great World War II generation. They are 'more interested in building things up than tearing them down.' Students in high school place great importance on being like everybody else. Everybody wants to wear the same clothes—to be accepted. They're playing follow the follower rather than follow the leader, or be the leader. So when it comes to picking a college and picking a career, rather than playing to their own strengths, they're trying to be one of the crowd, which is probably one of the tragedies of American youth today.

The bottom line is they don't know how to make decisions. They don't know how to set goals. They need our help.

Chapter 1: My story

COLLEGE ROULETTE

"I am the way and the truth and the life."

JOHN 14:4

"I had ambition not only to go farther than any man had ever been before, but as far as it was possible for a man to go."

CAPTAIN JAMES COOK

Changing Majors Seven Times at Six Colleges

Part of where my passion for self-determination came from was growing up in Maine as an only child. Although they loved me dearly, my parents didn't really have a lot of experience on how to get me through the process. So I kind of did what a lot of kids do today: started off with pre-med, then once I hit the wall with organic chemistry, I thought, "This is no fun." I grew up loving the ocean in Maine, so I thought, "Gee, maybe marine biology might be a good fit," and after that I tried aquaculture engineering. I ended up changing my major seven times attending six different colleges, which when you're paying $2,000 a year is not bad, but would be devastating at today's cost of $40,000 or upwards of $60,000 for elite schools like the Harvards and Yales of the world.

Why Did I Get into the Financial Planning Field?

As long as I can remember, I've had this burning desire to help people. After having changed my major seven times at six different colleges as an undergrad, I didn't want to repeat the same pattern in my career. In case you're wondering, the majors were:

1.   Health physics

2.   Pre-med

3.   Marine biology

4.   Aquaculture engineering

5.   Biology

6.   Short stint as a monk

7.   Education

When I finished grad school with a degree in what was basically theology, I met my wife, got married, worked as a guidance counselor here in Illinois, and realized it wasn't what I wanted to do. I didn't know what I wanted to do, and I definitely knew I did not want to repeat in my working life what I had done in my college life. I did some research and I found a local company called Career Vision, which is a division of a nonprofit organization called the Ball Foundation.

Because of their unique approach using aptitude tests in addition to interest exams and personality profiles, I decided to go through the process, and when my results came back they suggested I look into financial planning for several reasons: I had a desire to help people, and I would also be good at sales and training. A big surprise was my math scores. My two highest aptitudes were math, and my scores were almost off the chart. I pointed this out to my counselor Peg Hendershot, who has since become the director and who has been an incredible resource for me and my firm. I told her it had to be a mistake. I had two tough nuns in 8th grade and freshman year of high school, and I've hated math ever since. Peg assured me that, although related, high school and college math and the math used in financial planning were not the same thing. So just because I struggled with calculus in college did not mean I wouldn't succeed as a planner.

It turns out that the type of math and analytical skills used in financial planning was like breathing for me. So combining the math scores, my desire to help people, and my aptitudes for training and sales, financial planning was ideal.

That being said, however, I will admit that my first two years in this field were miserable for a lot of reasons. The track record for success in the financial services field is dismal. On average, after four years in the business, only 10 percent of those who started are still ticking. I stuck it out, though, and now I am blessed to say I have had the same career and the same wife for more than 25 years. (And no, Career Vision did not help me pick my wife!)

I first worked for a large national insurance company for about four years. For those of you parents who are looking to work with a college planner, be careful who he or she works for because remember, the only way the majority of financial advisors earn a living is by selling you something. The danger of working for large insurance companies that carry their own proprietary products is:

1) No matter what the problem, this company's products is the solution, and

2) No matter what the problem, life insurance is the solution. I'm sure you've all heard the expression, "If the

only tool you have is a hammer, then everything you see looks like a nail."

After five years of purgatory I ultimately started my own firm so I could charge fair fees and be compensated for my expertise and not for my ability to sell products. I really enjoy the independence, so when I do need to use products for my families I don't get compensated more for using one product than another. When I worked for the large insurance company, I was paid higher commissions for using this company's products versus other products. I think that is an incredible temptation for the advisor, and I truly believe it does a real disservice to the industry when people are compensated that way.

I decided to create Lighthouse College Financial Planning because of my own struggles during high school, having had no idea what I was doing as far as preparing for college and making a lot of bad decisions—basically having no compass heading, no direction, nothing. Originally, I wanted to provide parents with an understanding of the college financial aid process. Then I realized that even though we help the parents, the students still had no idea what they were doing. So I started counseling the students on a one-on-one basis. This grew to the point where I began bringing in outside guidance counselors on staff.

I started Lighthouse College Financial Planning in 2003 partly because of my oldest daughter's impending graduation in 2004 and also because I have this innate need to always improve things. I've got this burning drive to be the best at whatever I do. It drives my staff crazy, but in my mind it's like that famous line that Morgan Freeman says in *Shawshank Redemption*, "Either you're busy living, or you're busy dying." If we're not improving, we're getting worse. I always want to be better than the competition; there's a little bit of a competitive streak in me, but I think it really serves our client families well, which is why we get a lot of referrals, and lots of kudos and appreciation for the work we do.

The thing that gives me the most joy from what I do, is knowing we prevented parents and students from making the same mistakes I made before, and during, and after my college career. There is another line from a the movie called *P.S. I Love You* where the mother is talking to her recently widowed daughter and says, "The second worst thing that can happen to a parent is for the child to make the same mistakes that you did." So making sure my own four children and the families we work with avoid making the same financial and academic errors I did, and knowing that I have changed their world for the better, are huge motivators for me.

We have helped hundreds of students prepare for college using the same mantra: "1 major, 1 college, 4 years, and then off the family payroll." We have also helped parents figure out the best way to pay for college. We have a great track record of saving people money — an average of $40,000 to $60,000 per student just in the financial aid process. So I take a tremendous amount of pride in the work we do.

As you will see in later chapters, the timeline and work it takes to get students to find the right school and career makes for a lengthy process. It's a marathon, not a sprint. We have built the Lighthouse college planning process based on the concept of a three-legged stool: (1) career planning and school selection, (2) financial aid, and finally (3) the financial planning process. Unfortunately, most of the families who come into our office have only used one of the legs. And like any stool, if one of the legs is loose or missing, the stool wobbles and can even topple over. Later on, in the chapter called "The Good, the Bad and the Ugly," I'll give several examples of families who have toppled. Stay tuned.

Chapter 2

TOP 10 COLLEGE PLANNING MISTAKES

"Tell it to your children, and your children to their children, and their children to the next generation."

JOEL 1:3

"One door closes, another opens; but we stare so long and so regretfully upon the closed door that we do not see the one which has opened for us."

ALEXANDER GRAHAM BELL

I'm often asked what are the biggest mistakes families make when it comes to planning for college. I think they fall into two categories. There's the financial side, the hard cost, and then there's the soft costs. Let's start with some of the larger and more common mistakes.

1) The biggest mistake I see is waiting too long to start the college planning process. We start working with parents when their children are in 8th grade because that's a

good time to start adequately saving and to identify the best school-career choices. But as a rule we generally work with about 70 seniors per year. It's amazing the number of high school seniors who will show up at my office after September of their senior year. All through senior year they come into my office saying "please help me." It's like tying one hand behind my back — I can certainly help them, but would have been a lot easier, a lot more fruitful, and a lot less expensive if they would have started this process much earlier. I tell every family in my office that they are on a Titanic cruise. I am also on it. The problem is that in the real story the lookouts didn't see the iceberg, until the Titanic was only about a half mile away. When you have a ship that big moving that fast, there's not much you can do. There is going to be a collision, there is going to be a lot of damage. It's the same way with college. The closer you are to college or retirement, the closer you are to that iceberg. As a result you will have to make a more drastic course change, adjusting your lifestyle, sacrificing certain school choices, or whatever it is. Having enough time to plan is crucial to your success.

2) Another top mistake is the parents choosing their child's career for him or her. We want our kids to find *their* dream jobs, so it is very important not to choose your child's

career. That should be a decision your child makes solely on his or her own.

3) A third mistake is pushing your student to go to a particular school because you went to that school. Or picking a school for many of the reasons I've heard over the years such as: My best friend is going there. My boyfriend is going there. My girlfriend is going there. Mom and Dad went there. Mom and Dad didn't go there. It's a big school. It's a small school. It's close to home. It's far away from home. It's sunny. It's cold. It's warm. I like the basketball team. I like the football team. I like the mascot. I like the mascot they used to have. It's in the city. It's in the country. It's near the ocean (this one is acceptable ☺). All of those reasons are not good reasons to pick a school.

4) I see people make assumptions that a big-ten school or a well-known school is going to give them a better shot at getting a job. This is absolutely false. There are a lot of schools that are not as well known, but have phenomenal academic programs. My own daughter, for example, went to Florida Institute of Technology. Nobody I knew except for engineers had ever heard of it before. The year she graduated, they ended up placing 100 percent of the ocean engineers who graduated. Again, people look for

what's familiar, what they know, instead of thinking outside the box and looking for what works.

5) Two big related mistakes parents make are thinking either that they can't afford to pay for school or that they will have no problem paying when in fact they have major cash-flow issues. Or, they may think, "I don't need to worry about school. I'll let my child pay for it." But their children's access to money is extremely limited.

6) Another mistake centers around expected family contribution or "EFC." As I'll explain later, that's the amount of money the government says you can afford to pay every year before qualifying for need-based aid. Here parents may be thinking, "Well, I make too much money to qualify for financial aid." That is absolutely not true. We usually have several families each year who make well into the six figures and have had their kids get anywhere from half to three-quarters to full rides, and that obviously has nothing to do with their income.

7) Thinking, for example, your child is not a good enough athlete to get an athletic scholarship, is a mistake. Again, this assumption is absolutely false, especially when you are looking at your Division II, Division III, and NAIA schools. The first question they are going to ask your student is not what her sports statistics are, but what is her GPA. So good students who are also good athletes

will discover there's lots of money out there. This topic will be discussed in our next book, due out later this year.

8) Another mistake is **assuming going to a community college first is a bad idea**. Many parents who come through my office look down their noses at the suggestion of their child attending a community college the first two years. They think the education is sub-par or inadequate. While this may be true if you are comparing a community college to an elite school like a Harvard or Notre Dame, such a sweeping generalization should not be applied to all schools.

A community college can be a great choice for those who don't know what they want to do. It can also be wise when your child might not have the level of maturity to go away to college or when attending a four-year school might be too much of a financial burden.

9) **Choosing not to take honors classes or advanced placement (AP) classes.** Some high-school guidance counselors recommend students not take honors classes so they will have a higher GPA. Although there are a few colleges that will not accept the weighting of an honors class, I have yet to find a student who didn't appreciate the extra rigor involved as a real preparation for college-level academics.

Many students will find the amount of reading material they need to go through in college on a daily basis analogous to drinking from a fire hose. So taking higher level classes in high school will ease the transition/ burden of college-level academics.

10) **Applying to to only one or two schools.** When you do this it doesn't give you opportunities to leverage the schools against each other. Also, it is not unusual for students to change their minds as late as their junior or even senior year. If you've only applied to one school and change your mind, you're outta luck.

Also, financial aid packages are going to vary from school to school. One of our seniors this year was offered a full ride at an elite school in Virginia and yet had to pay full price for his top pick school in North Carolina. He also had two phenomenal offers from two Midwestern universities. If he had only applied to his dream school, his family would be stuck with a $41,000 college bill instead of $0 out of pocket cost for a great school. Since he's going to study political science and will need to go to grad school, the money they saved for his B.A. can be applied to his master's degree (as long as he cooperates with Mom and Dad ☺)

Bonus Point: Students having no Plan B. For students a Plan B would look like having a double major or a major-minor. For example, someone who wants to be a professional musician should consider getting a degree in music education or music business. Someone who wants to teach history should also get dual certification to teach math or science. Recently in our own school district a position for a history teacher opened up and there were 1700 applicants. At the same time there were shortages for math and science teachers. Having a backup major would provide an alternative path, a "Plan B" that could be used if one path doesn't work out. Another example would be my son, Michael, who is graduating with a double major in civil and environmental engineering. While the civil degree is helpful, the environmental degree is in more demand currently. Again, if one plan doesn't work, Michael has his "Plan B" as a safety net.

Chapter 3: Planning for College

THE THREE-LEGGED STOOL

"That one is like a person building a house, who dug deeply and laid the foundation on rock; when the flood came, the river burst against that house but could not shake it because it had been well built."

LUKE 6:48

"A genius! For thirty- seven years I've practiced fourteen hours a day, and now they call me a genius!"

PABLO SARASATE

If you look at college planning using the analogy of a three-legged stool, it will help you better understand the important parts of the plan you should address. What I tell my clients is to think about a stool with only two legs. Without the third leg, it is unstable and will fall over. So too will financial planning for college if a three-part approach is not taken.

I recommend the following process: (1) career planning and school selection, (2) financial aid, and (3) financial planning. The key is to have all three legs of the "stool" present to create a successful process.

Most families focus on school selection. They may look at careers, they may look at financial aid, but almost everyone ignores financial planning, and almost no one really looks at all three legs of the stool.

If you're going through this process and you're trying to find a professional to work with, I encourage you to find a financial planner, not just a financial advisor, and find someone who is a Certified College Planning Specialist. Let me explain the difference between a financial advisor and a financial planner.

In the state of Illinois, a financial advisor differs from a financial planner in a couple of key areas: A financial advisor only has limited fiduciary responsibility and can only be paid by selling you something, and. Also, a financial planner, which is what I am, is somewhat like an attorney or an accountant. We have a greater fiduciary responsibility, which means we always have to do what is in our client's best interest.

A financial planner can charge fees, like an attorney or an accountant. When you are paying a fee to someone, you expect to get professional, objective advice and not have to worry about, "Gee, is this person doing what's best for me, or what's best for him or her." Working with someone who is a Certified College Planning Specialist guarantees you are working with someone who is trained in all three areas – school selection, financial aid, and financial planning — and is also required by the National Institute of Certified College Planners to have continuing education hours every single year.

Career Planning and School Selection

A little planning now can save a lot of money in the future. Research your child's career choices first. The career choices will determine the major, the major will determine the school, and the choice of school will determine the costs of college. This part of your plan—this leg of the stool—needs to be done in this order.

Unfortunately, many people go through this step backwards. They start with the college costs. This puts price before need. For example, if someone would say here, "We can only afford $22,000 a year for college," several universities in Illinois fit this criteria. But let's say the student wants a major in bio-medical engineering or entrepreneurship. None of these schools has either of these majors.

Most students don't consider what they are good at versus what they are interested in, or the educational requirements (for instance, seven or eight years of schooling if the student plans to go to medical school). We suggest that the student and parents discover these things through testing and job shadowing, which we will discuss in a future chapter.

Next, once you know your career choice, this will define the major you should choose in school. Again, make sure you are both interested and able to pursue that major. For example, if you want to major in engineering but you are not good in math, then you need to step back and re-evaluate. Maybe an alternative would be an engineering tech degree, which is only three years and not as math-intensive. It is also more hands-on and less theoretical, which may fit the personalities of certain people.

In this third planning step where the major determines the school choices, you will find schools don't offer "all" majors. For example, in the medical field practically every school has a pre-med program. This doesn't mean they all offer nursing, physical therapy, exercise physiology, occupational therapy, or speech pathology. Here, you will need to connect the major to the school choice.

Finally, in the fourth step the school choice will determine your college cost. This could result in a situation where some choices are beyond your financial abilities or you opt to send your child to an out-of-state school that is less expensive or some other plan B. Here you might work with your child having him take out loans for a portion of the college expenses or having him go to a junior college for two years and transfer to a more expensive school in his third year. An additional note here is that your child may earn a scholarship at a junior college. If your child is on the honor roll he or she is eligible to join Phi Theta Kappa, the honor society for junior colleges. Then the four-year schools he or she would transfer to for junior and senior year may provide scholarships to transfer students. (Note: You have to research these colleges to make sure they will transfer credits as some do and some don't.)

All four of our children cost between $11,000 and $13,000 annually to go to $40,000-plus four-year schools. This was first because I found schools with money that would pay my children to go there. Also, because I knew the strategies and techniques to secure help with college expenses, I was able to save a substantial amount for each child's education. This book will help you do the same.

If you are willing to take the time to go through the planning process, you will realize substantial results. You may have a plan A in mind, but you may also need to consider plan B or even plan C.

What Makes Lighthouse Planning Different From Other College Planners?

When a family walks through our doors and says, "We want your help. We want to work with you," we might suggest they go through the Career Vision process, depending on the age of the student. But let's start with 8th graders. For this age group we actually have a softer program called Career Cruising that most high schools in our area in Illinois purchase and also Naviance which is a phenomenal tool used by a few schools in our area.

We start by talking to the student, finding out her grades, looking at her report cards, considering the class schedule she has signed up for. We make suggestions on the next semester's classes and find out what she is interested in because we want to make her as marketable as possible. If we have a student interested in going into law, then we suggest that they join the debate team or forensics. For somebody who wants to go into engineering or math, we will see if he can join a mathletes team. Or perhaps he might take a wood class, drafting class, or some type of tech class at school. We work to get students involved in programs or extracurricular activities related to what they are going to do.

Students come into our office and spend some time with the guidance counselors one-on-one. We always require the parents to be there because we've learned the hard way that if you give little Suzy or little Johnny some homework, most of them will not get it done. We provide them with a tracking calendar, a binder with a CD of sample essays, six pages of questions to interview the schools with, and we give them a calendar to mark off what they need to be doing week by week, month by month. The parents get a copy and we keep a copy so everybody stays on track.

We also help by offering a mock interview workshop. We will invite a group of students in and videotape them as if they are being interviewed by a college. Some of the interviews are for admissions, some for additional scholarships. Then we give them a DVD copy of the interview so they can see how they did. I like to think of our counselors as your child's personal college success coaches; they are here to work with students one-on-one and provide that personal touch.

What I do for the parents, on the other hand, is get to know the families, talk about the kids, learning about any characteristics we need to take into consideration during the college planning process for that child. We usually have several students every year with either ADD or ADHD, and if it is severe enough we want to find a supportive college environment that can handle these situations. Some schools will actually knock on your student's door and make sure he or she gets out of bed to get to class on time.

We will work with the parents, finding out about their past financial history, if they've worked with a financial advisor or a financial planner before, what their experience has been like. I will ask them if they are coachable, which is crucial, and get an emotional response to how they feel about getting ready for college, and also getting ready for retirement. We take a snapshot of their financials, and then the next meeting we fill out a cash flow spreadsheet so we can start determining how much the parents can put aside per month to pay for college. These are available on our site which is listed at the end of the book.

We will also look at retirement. If a family tells me they can save $2,000 a month for college, but it means they have to work till they are 80 until they can retire, that's not a good idea. So I always look at the whole picture, to make sure all the pieces of the puzzle fit together. We will look at what can be borrowed, what they already have in investments, how much they can put aside per month, and then we produce a college funding spreadsheet showing year-by-year how much they can afford to pay per child, per year, adjusted for inflation (typically we use six percent). This way Mom and Dad know how much is affordable for them, and little Suzy and little Johnny know how much they will have to pay. The parents can then go back to the kids and say, "This is how much we can afford to pay, and if the school costs more than that, either you have to find a school that will pay you to go there, or you will have to borrow it, work for it, or a combination of the three". This way everybody knows what's going on, and there are no surprises. Everyone gets to accomplish his or her dreams without crashing into each other's "icebergs".

If the parents plan on borrowing the money for college, my goal as a professional is to make sure they are debt-free by the time they retire. So we will look at ways to pay off their debt early. Sometimes we utilize a software program, and other times it's just putting a budget and spreadsheet together, especially if parents have existing debt such as credit cards. We then put together a schedule so they know when they will be debt-free.

Sometimes I get asked this question: "How did you send four kids to college without being a multi-millionaire?" Well, that is a great question. One thing that helped me was being a business owner. Number two was being a college financial planner and knowing the rules of the game. The financial aid rules were made for two types of people: individuals, and business owners. The loopholes that are available for business owners are incredible. As a business owner I set up different retirement and deferred compensation plans which did not have to appear in the college financial aid forms and which paid my children, especially when they were younger.

The Right Financial Plan

So we have the right career choice, the right college, and financial aid. The next thing is the right financial plan. For every family who comes into my office, I present to them a spreadsheet that will show how much borrowing it's going to cost to send their child to his or her dream school. For a family with three kids, if they borrow their way through this, just going to a school like the University of Illinois which this year is about $30,000, you can expect that the total loan cost will be somewhere between $500,000 and $750,000. That is outrageous. Every year I'm amazed at the number of families who still decide to pay for school that way. No wonder the US economy is in such bad shape.

Although we send our kids to school so they can achieve their dreams, it's important that Mom and Dad achieve theirs as well. What you don't want to have happen is for your kid to be saddled with so much debt that they're moving back in with you after they graduate. Or you would have to move in with them when you retire. One of the saddest things I saw was one of my daughter's best friends who wanted to go into teaching, and went to Illinois State. She was responsible for taking out all of the loans, graduated, got some offers to teach, but had so much debt she couldn't afford to rent an apartment or make a car payment, so she ended up teaching at one of the local parochial schools because she could live at home, take the bus, walk, or ride a bike from home to school. That's not what we really want for our kids. So you want to make sure you develop the right financial plan.

Having a financial plan is crucial if you're planning on borrowing and being debt-free by retirement. Even with loans and scholarships, it is still going to be a significant amount of out-of-pocket cost for the parents, and they need to figure out where this money is coming from.

I would say in general that as a parent you definitely do not want to take money out of your retirement plans to pay for college. Unless you have sat down with your financial planner and been shown that you are ahead of the curve—way ahead of the curve—I would treat your retirement money like your marriage vows. Sacred. Do not violate that money at all.

The Counselor Connection

I mentioned earlier we have counselors in our office. All of them are master's level or master's candidates in counseling. The counselor's job is to get the students moving toward a career and get them involved in activities that relate to their chosen career. Maybe a better title for them is a college success coach. As I said earlier, if a student wants to be an attorney, have her join the debate team, join forensics, or speech club. For someone who wants to get into the medical field, I was given great advice by a physician for each of those students to become a CNA, a certified nurse's assistant, so they can actually work in a hospital and find out what it's like. Better to find out now than get through two years of medical school and decide you don't like it. When the students and parents aren't seeing eye to eye on things, the counselors really try to work with everyone to come up with a game plan everybody can live with.

Why work with a financial planner instead of doing it yourself? Ask yourself these questions: Do you have the time and the discipline to make this a second career? Do you have the temperament? Do you have the experience? From the standpoint of knowing where to look, knowing where to find the schools, knowing how to interview the schools, we stand ready to help. This is the information we pass on so that we can find the schools your child will thrive at academically, environmentally, and financially.

As I mentioned earlier, the way to start selecting the right college is by finding the right major. When you consider that 37 percent of college freshman don't go back, 33 percent transfer schools, and 57 percent take up to six years to get a degree, you can see that too many students make a decision based on their interests and not their aptitudes.

Another consideration when choosing a major is whether your child will be able to pay the bills when he or she graduates. Be sure to look at things like the growth projection for a specific career. I always encourage students to have a plan A, plan B, and possibly a plan C. I had one young lady come into the office a couple years ago. Her plan A was that she wanted to be a professional dancer. Plan B was that she wanted to open up her own dance school. I had to ask her what the likelihood was of that actually happening and being able to support herself. It isn't my intention to deprive anyone of their dreams in life, but I want students to be realistic.

An article that appeared in the *Wall Street Journal* last year stated that as a result of the recession, it would take the average college graduate five years to get a job in their major. Let's think about that. If I had been invited to write a part II of that article it would have been this: If those predictions are true, then we're essentially graduating a bunch of burger flippers or supermarket stockers. Certainly necessary professions, but probably not what you intended for your student. The more horrifying thought is this: let's say the five years have gone by and your student's field of choice has now opened up. Your son or daughter goes in for the interview; the HR person looks at their resume and asks two crucial questions: (1)"What have you been doing for the last five years?" and (2) "Are you current in your field?" One of my wife's relatives who had immigrated to the United States during the recession in the 1970s simply could not find a job in civil engineering. He finally gave up and got a job driving a cab in Chicago. When the engineering field finally opened up a few years later, he was woefully behind in current best practices and technology.

I'm already seeing this happen with some of our clients' students. One of our students who graduated in 2010 with a degree in mechanical engineering is currently working for a swimming pool company. Another young lady graduated in 2010 with a degree in interior design from a school with a great reputation in that field, and is working at the local supermarket. A way to deal with this challenge is to have either a double major or have a major and minor like our daughter Shireen, who majored in marketing and minored in communications.

You want to have a plan A and B not only when choosing a major, but also when selecting the right college. I remember one student who came into my office three years ago. She was a bright young lady, had a 32 on her ACT, a 4.0 GPA, and the only school she had applied to was the University of Illinois, which has a great reputation for their engineering program. When I asked her why she picked that school, she said that it was the number three engineering school in the country. When I asked her who told her that, she replied that U of I had.

I pointed out to her that *US News and World Report* rated them as number four in the country for *public* schools. Basically, *US News and World Report* sends out a big questionnaire, and then U of I (along with all the other schools that are ranked by US News) sends it back with a big check. So all of the data is self-reported. "Wouldn't Harvey Mudd, MIT, Rose Hullman, Virginia Tech, Stanford, Cal Tech, Georgia Tech, and the like disagree with U of I saying they're number three?" I asked her.

Then I asked her how much she thought it would cost for a degree at U of I. She wasn't sure. "Well, let's assume it would be about $25,000 a year." She said, "Well, that would be $100,000."

"Well, not really," I said. "Typically it's very difficult to get into some of the classes, so you really need to count on getting your degree in five years."

"That would be $125,000," she responded.

"Let's take a look at this other school," I suggested. Before she had come in, I contacted another university, talked to the dean, and gave her the young lady's stats. With scholarships the approximate cost per year was going to be about $8,000 to go to a $37,000-a-year school. Not only that, but 90 percent of its engineering students graduated in four years. And they had a five-year master's degree, which as a good student she would likely be able to get funded through a grad or teaching assistantship.

So I turned this back to the student, pointing out that it would cost approximately $45,000 for a five-year master's degree. I told her that most firms would prefer she have a masters degree before hiring. "So you can get a five-year master's degree for $45,000 versus a five-year bachelor's degree for $125,000," I said. I mentioned that both schools were well-ranked and she would get a job when she got out.

Now without reading farther ahead, which school do you think she picked? Well, if you guessed U of I you'd be right. "Because it's the number three engineering school in the country," she explained. Everything I'd said had just totally gone into some void. This illustrates that you want to start this process early because the longer you wait, the more your children begin to put on blinders like on a race horse, closing themselves off to the other opportunities that are out there.

Various Parents' Plans for College
[A SUMMARY]

Plan A: They have discretionary income and assets to pay for school

Plan B: Parents and/or students have to borrow money to pay for college.

Plan C: A lifestyle change where either the parents decrease their expenses to pay for college (e.g. giving up daily lattes) or increase their income. Many moms of the families I work with are at home or working part-time. Mom here may have to go back to the workplace.

The other option is pushing off retirement for a few years.

Plan B is ok as long as the student's loan is no higher than his or her first-year salary. Someone who is going to be a teacher with an income of $35-40,000 a year should not have $60,000 in total loans. He or she will end up either moving back home with Mom and Dad or living off of ramen noodles and peanut butter!

Also, as I mentioned earlier, I don't have a problem with the parents paying for their child or children's college as long as they are going to be debt-free when they retire.

Various Students' Plans for College

Plan A: Getting to go to their dream school.

Plan B: Going to a good school that offers them money to attend.

Plan C: Going to a local school within driving distance and commuting.

Plan D: Going to a community college for a year or two and transferring.

I would rather see a student go to junior college for two years and then transfer to an excellent school than go to a mediocre school for four years. The bottom line here is to be open and flexible, and to remove the blinders from your kids and yourselves to look at alternative possibilities.

Chapter 4: Getting a Smart Start

LESSONS FROM THE TITANIC

"The child grew and became strong, filled with
wisdom; and the favor of God was upon him."

LUKE 2:40

"Are you going places, or just being taken?"

H.F. HENRICHS

Avoid a Titanic Journey

I referred to The Titanic earlier, but now I will go even deeper.
The *Titanic* is one of the most memorable, horrific, and avoidable
disasters in history. One of the major points was that the
lookouts did not see the iceberg until it was a half-mile away.
By the time they finally spotted it, there was literally nothing
they could have done except wait to hit the iceberg.

But if they had known the iceberg was out there before they
set sail from Southampton, England, all they would have had

to do was to change their course by a fraction of a degree and they would have missed it by miles. College planning is similar because the farther away you are from your "iceberg," the better opportunity you have to successfully plan for it.

Many people come in to see us in their child's junior year of high school. This is like the iceberg being only two miles away. They have procrastinated, and they are trying to avoid a disaster of biblical proportions. If they had started this process in middle school, or even better when their child was six, it would have been like the *Titanic* making a course correction around the iceberg when she left port in Southampton.

So imagine the vision of the *Titanic* as we move through planning that should start in grade school, or more specifically first grade when there is a much better opportunity to get your children building a healthy savings mindset and behavior.

This would mean having at least monthly meetings with your child to set up an allowance of which some portion is put back into a savings account. Borrowing a term from my colleague Steph Fuller, you might think of this as your child's 401Kid Plan. In fact, it wouldn't hurt when putting aside money to include some family contribution. For example a small portion could contribute to family expense such as mortgage, heating, cooling, etc.

Another idea here would be for you to match dollars for their savings, as many employers do with 401Ks. In many employers' experience, a number of employees do not contribute to their 401Ks unless their companies match contributions. Over the years I have seen that in families where parents are not good with their finances, their kids are not good at math and have no concept of the value of money.

It is not only in financial matters that an early start makes a difference to college and career success. Many students are not good readers. I hear this substantiated from my wife, who teaches gifted children. We have researched and discovered that the students who do the most poorly in testing do not have good reading skills. It is found that students who typically have parents reading to them and who develop a love for reading not only have better test scores but also find it easier to adjust to the demands of rigorous college classes.

Also, socializing your child and getting him or her involved in extracurricular activities makes a positive difference to success. Expand your child's horizons. Have your kids try different things. If children's only experiences in life are about what goes on in their home or school, they are missing out a lot. These "life skills" may seem soft, but they are strong in the success they can yield for your child and the satisfaction you will feel as your child excels beyond his or her current environment.

At Lighthouse we are continually learning more about what makes a good academic and financial start in life. We share these ideas with our clients and will share them with you on our website to help build that good practice of savings.

Middle School—Spreading Your Wings Even Farther

Whether it's sports or music or whatever, this is the time to help your children really expand their horizons. If you have a good student, try to get him or her involved in accelerated/challenge/gifted classes during middle school. Don't think your child is beyond you spending time with him or her.

This is time we like to see families come in to see us—right around 8th grade, or even younger if possible. Here your child is around thirteen or fourteen. You have spent time working with him or her to develop good spending habits. We help you further build those habits and grow your college nest egg, setting that foundation over the course of five years that will ready your child for the rest of his or her life.

Creating a Savings Mentality Early On

One of my colleagues, Stephanie, is a top business executive with a Fortune 500 company working across 54 countries around the world. She has a great family and is one of seven children who has learned valuable life lessons on money management through games her father taught her and her siblings. For example her dad would play a game called Easter Egg and another called Disposable Income with her and her siblings to help them learn how to manage money better. Her father was a successful entrepreneur who wanted his children to learn all about money management in a fun way. He also wanted to teach his children to think for themselves.

Remember those plastic Easter eggs that many parents would put around the house for family Easter egg hunts? Stephanie's father used to put slips of paper into the eggs with questions they needed to answer about converting foreign currency into U.S. currency. For example, the slips might ask them to convert five British Pounds Sterling or 30 Dominican Pesos or 20 Swiss Francs into U.S. currency. Stephanie and her siblings had to go to a conversion list their father cut out from the *Wall Street Journal*. The purpose of the game was to learn the value of money, but it was also fun and challenging.

Another game, called Disposable Income, was all about spending money wisely, allocating dollars for personal expenses, taxes, and savings, and only then using the leftover amount to spend as one would want. For example, they would get $100 and their father would say, "You owe Uncle Sam $5, so now you have $95. But you also left the lights on in the house, so you owe $10 for the electricity bill. Additionally, you were on the phone, so you owe $7 for your phone usage. Finally, you have to save at least 50% of your income. Now, whatever you have left is your disposable income."

Stephanie says with great passion, "The purpose of this game was about using our money wisely. This game really helped me become a great saver. I think it is always important to know how to live within your means. Also, I believe that knowledge is power. If you have the knowledge as to how to make money, keep money, and grow your savings, then you are able to work through anything." What have you done to teach your child the purpose of money? It's never too late. Start today.

Additionally, check out the Appendix where we provide you and your children with comprehensive checklists to prepare them for college.

Chapter 5

"IT AIN'T EASY BEING GREEN"

"How varied are your works, LORD! In
wisdom you have wrought them all."

PSALM 90:12

"You can always tell an adolescent,
but you can't tell them much."

ANON

So, What Do You Want to Be When You Grow Up?

BY LAYLA

Think back to your earliest responses to the question, "What do you want to be when you grow up?" You may have dreamed of being a cowboy, movie star, fireman, priest, or flight attendant. Of the thousands of choices before us, these responses evolve as we mature. We discover that some jobs are more lucrative than others; thus becoming a doctor or a lawyer seems more appealing. We come to realize that some career choices have limited opportunities in our society, such as the cowboy. But most importantly, we come to know ourselves better, our strengths, weaknesses, and passions.

I think back many years ago to the career goals I recorded in my first grade "All About Me" booklet. I wanted to be a movie star or a singer just like Julie Andrews. Now that I've happily settled into a teaching career, I still strive to emulate those traits of a singer and actress I so admired as a first-grader. As I grew up, I realized that I have many important things to share with the world, and that I am energized by dialogue with others. I love being in front of and with groups of people with a common cause. And then there is something magical about the positive, charismatic way that so many of Andrews's film characters transformed the people and world around them.

The other seemingly obvious nugget of wisdom I now realize is that I don't have to find a career that incorporates *all* of my interests and passions. I love singing, but I can enjoy that in my church choir. I enjoy gardening and the beauty of nature too, and that has prompted me to create outdoor activities and service projects with my students, but I really need to fulfill this interest in my own leisure time.

Each generation of young people journeys through similar transformations in their understanding of themselves and their career choices. When our young son, Michael, exuberantly announced his aspiration to be a garbage man, I held my tongue. Instead of instinctively blurting out the family "college goals sermon," I quietly nodded and smiled. Deep down, I knew that Michael admired the demonstration of brute physical strength and the obvious helpfulness of these men. Similarly, when our young Christopher confided that he was struggling between his desire to be a cowboy and a priest, I held back the laughter. How diametrically opposed these seemed. Yet, I also realized there were qualities in both that even a young child could admire: the brazen machismo of the cowboy and the spiritual leadership of the priest.

Actually, there are three very basic questions young people should ask themselves to consider the qualities that define them: (1) What do I love doing? (2) What is most important to me in life? and (3) What am I good at? The passions that bring meaning to our lives, along with our God-given abilities, come to a "meeting of the mind" as the college years approach. Amazingly, for some there seems to be a seamless match and a clear direction. But for many, choosing a career path can be a confusing and daunting task.

Too often it is the wrong questions that are being asked: (1) What is the most prestigious career I can enter? (2) Which careers earn the most money? and (3) What do others expect me to be? Young people who are raised with very high expectations for their future often feel constricted by these parameters and ignore their own passions. To be sure, these are the same high expectations that helped this young person ready him or herself for a promising future, but we must be careful to balance the lofty aspirations with opportunities that truly reflect the young person's interests and talents.

On the other hand, a different set of assumptions by young people and their families lead to low aspirations: (1) No one in our family has ever been successful in this career, so you probably won't be either. (2) If you don't enjoy every aspect of a career, you shouldn't pursue it. Or (3) You'll be safer in a career that you are very familiar with right now, not something you'll need to learn a great deal about. When a young person thinks this way or is surrounded by friends or family who do, it is difficult to aspire to the greatness in him or herself. Familiarity and/or fear of taking any risks in one's career search is greatly debilitating.

In both sets of misleading questions and assumptions, fear and the pressure to conform act as blinders to clear decision making. In addition to shedding those typical fears and pressures, young people must be reminded: There is no rule that says you cannot change or modify your career any number of times. That is the beauty of the search; it is part of a normal and glorious evolution in growing up and growing up again. If you talk with a room full of successful adults, you will inevitably find that most of them are not in the career they began in. In addition, most do not regret the earlier steps to their most recent choice; instead they are usually natural stepping stones of experience and exposure which prepared them more fully for their present career.

What *Do* I Want to Do With the Rest of My Life? [COLLEGE VIEW]

BY SHIREEN

Singer. Pianist. Baseball player. Model. Child psychologist. What do these professions have in common? Well, these were my career aspirations throughout grade school. Anyone who knows me would surely say that all of these careers are highly unattainable for me. Actually, it would be more accurate to say impossible (due to the fact that I didn't pursue singing, piano, or softball after fifth grade.)

Despite my early fanciful dreams of becoming a Celine Dion or female version of Sammy Sosa, I always kept one thing in mind: I would continue to search for something that fit me. It wasn't until my freshman year in high school that I started thinking seriously about my career path. During the winter break of that year I thought I had found the perfect solution.

When visiting my grandmother in Maine for Christmas, we were introduced to her neighbors, Stephanie and Jeffrey. It became evident to me that they were very well off, seeing that their three-floor house had been completely renovated. One day Jeffrey decided to give my sister and me a tour, and upon reaching the third floor of their home, we discovered something very interesting. Lining the shelves above the staircase were multiple antique medicine bottles. I recognized some of the names, but others were completely unknown to me. I began asking Jeffrey many questions, and he in turn shared with me everything I could want to know about his job as a pharmacist.

Within a week, my mind was set; I was going to become a pharmacist. I mean, why not? He answered in one way or another my most pressing concerns. My first concern was that I knew I needed to work with people. Solution: Of course I would be surrounded by people constantly! Clearly, everyone asks the local pharmacists the most important medicinal questions, and I could be like a modern-day *Dr. Quinn, Medicine Woman*. (Can you see my train of thought already?)

My second concern was my fierce opposition to taking any more math or science courses. Solution: From what it looks like, pharmacists don't need either. (I didn't realize that I would need to take chemistry, biology, and definitely calculus.)

My third and final concern was that I wanted to make a lot of money. Well, no problem finding that!

So as you can probably tell, my first attempts at finding a career were a bit naïve. After I did a little more research I quickly discovered that a job in the pharmaceutical field was definitely not what I was looking for. I had to take a step back from searching for jobs whose main point of attraction was money. I needed some time and direction to seek out my true interests, aptitudes, and aspirations.

When I was interested in becoming a pharmacist, I was right in thinking that I needed a job where I was in constant contact with others. My first step in the right direction was looking into the communications field. It was through researching this area that I truly discovered my need and great ability to work with people. Finally, I started down the right path to choose a career, but it still took a few months to work out the kinks. After career counseling and a deeper look at what I was searching for, I had made up my mind to study business. I need much of the same skills for business that I do for a major in communications, so I decided to do both. I finally settled on a major in marketing and a minor in communications, two fields that go hand in hand.

To be sure, very few of us are born knowing what we want to do. In fact, even fewer of us know what it is that will make us happy in our careers. There is no real way of getting around the trial-and-error nature of a career search. However, we can certainly do things to help keep us on the right track.

✔ **Get career counseling.** While we are searching for a career, career counselors do just that for a living: find people careers! With a counselor, you'll be able to put your personality, interests, and aptitudes together to help you make the right choice.

✔ **Find your strengths *and* weaknesses.** It may be easy for you to find what you're not the best at, but to pinpoint what you are really good at may be more difficult. Ask your teachers, friends, and parents to talk to you about what they see you thrive in and what they know is not your forte. The people who know you best can always be there to help.

✔ **Be open.** Just because you are Richard Henry V and all the other Richard Henry's have been corporate lawyers doesn't mean you have to follow the same path. You may not have ever considered your true calling.

Choosing a career is nothing if not difficult. Just remember as you are search that you are a changing, growing young person. Try looking ten to twenty years into your future and picturing yourself in your chosen career. Then get started interviewing, researching, and shadowing!

Thankfully, there are many tools at our disposal to help us through this process.

Career Assessment and Counseling Services

BY JOHN

Following is a set of different career assessments with explanations. They will help assess your child's career path, research majors, choose colleges, develop resumes and cover letters, and more.

Career Vision: Career Vision is a not-for-profit research and consulting organization dedicated to helping families and their students understand their unique aptitudes, or natural strengths, and teaching them how to make great education and career choices as they transition through high school and college. This comprehensive and individualized service uses the "Ball Aptitude Battery"® in conjunction with other critical assessments such as interests, values, and personality, along with a private family conference, either in person or via teleconference, to support informed college major and career decision- making at any stage of life.

Naviance Succeed: Allows students to make real strides in researching colleges and making informed decisions from the comfort of home, while allowing their counselors to stay abreast of their progress and communicate with them electronically. Naviance Succeed promotes college and career readiness through increased collaboration, rigor, and transparency. It is a comprehensive online solution designed to achieve the desired outcomes while measuring progress against milestones.

Career Cruising: Is an industry-leading online career guidance and planning system. People of all ages use the tools to find the right career, explore education and training options, and build their own portfolio. The add-on products allow schools the ability to manage their course selection process, communities to meet their workforce development needs, and students to prepare for the ACT/SAT.

ASVAB: The Armed Services Vocational Aptitude Battery is the most widely used multiple-aptitude test battery in the world. As an aptitude test, the ASVAB measures your strengths, weaknesses, and potential for future success. The ASVAB also provides you with career information for various civilian and military occupations and is an indicator for success in future endeavors whether you choose to go to college, vocational school, or a military career.

Myers-Briggs Type Indicator: Is a personality inventory that can assist you with career planning at every stage: from your choices of subjects and majors in school to choosing your first career to advancing in your organization or changing careers later in life. The MBTI assesses psychological preferences in how people perceive the world and make decisions.

While one can certainly utilize many of the above resources on one's own, this cannot be compared to the support and expertise offered by a reputable career assessment and counseling service. These services often begin with a personal interview to assess the needs of each particular client.

Typically, your child will first be given a battery of aptitude tests. These tests go far beyond the verbal and mathematical tests that schools use to predict academic success. A comprehensive battery of aptitude tests might include tests that assess ten to twenty different skills such as vocabulary comprehension, finger dexterity (fine motor skills), physical endurance (measured by the ability to grip an object tightly for a given length of time), short-term memory, or even spatial aptitude (measured by the ability to assemble three-dimensional puzzles).

Later, the skills in which your child demonstrates a high aptitude are linked with appropriate careers. For example, dentistry, surgery, playing musical instruments, some assembly-line work, some office machine operations, and laboratory work all require high levels of finger dexterity. Spatial ability is also required in a good number of diverse professionals, such as mechanics, technicians, doctors, dentists, architects, and fashion designers.

Listen to Your Mom

BY LAYLA

When your children are wrestling with important decisions such as a career direction, it is very important that they talk openly to the members of their family. While many young people preparing for college want desperately to be independent as they forge their own path in the world, it is vital for them to reflect on their journey thus far. Their family is not only aware of their abilities, interests, and passions; they know their children's habits, moods, and unspoken desires. *Your children should not underestimate the value of family members' observations and suggestions in continuing their education.* Of course, in listening to these suggestions they will need to sift through any positive and negative bias they have toward certain careers. The key is to *listen* and reflect.

I remember years ago when my own mother suggested that I consider teaching as a career. Both of my parents had taught, and I had just been exposed to thirteen years of teachers since kindergarten! I wanted something different, exciting, and more importantly, something that *I* had discovered on my own. Finally, after two changes of my major in college, I began to think of teaching again, not so much as a familiar option to fall back on, but as an exciting opportunity to serve and inspire young people. Don't miss out on this valuable insight that can help you put the pieces of the puzzle together.

Chapter 6: Marketability Mistakes

MADISON AVENUE
GOES TO COLLEGE

"Plans Made After Advice Succeed."

PROVERBS 20:18

"Anybody can give advice – the trouble comes
in finding someone interested in using it."

ANON

Pre-college students consume an enormous amount of energy finding "the right college," but the best way to open up their opportunities is for *them* to become the best students they can. Perhaps another way to put it is that they need to become the right type of students for the college they want to get into. They need to hone their talents: putting forth their best efforts in high school literally will open up scores, if not hundreds of additional college options. While high school juniors and seniors are investigating colleges, these same institutions of higher learning are searching for students who match the academic level and vision of each school. They seek young men and women who will enhance the learning and extracurricular involvement for the whole student body, thereby increasing the value and prestige of the institution. If I were to put a Madison Avenue spin on it, I would title this section, "Increasing the Marketability of Your Student."

I would say that most schools fall into three basic categories with regard to the qualifications they look for in a student. Schools in the first category, which include many state universities and also many elite schools, basically look for GPA, ACT, and class rank. An example would be a client's daughter we were working with who was the valedictorian at her school. She had a 27 ACT, 4.0+ GPA (weighted) and was a nationally ranked figure skater, yet she ended up getting deferred by one of the more prestigious state universities in Illinois. Obviously, the fact that this young lady had an incredible work ethic and talent outside of scholastics didn't carry much weight with this particular school. Similarly, when my son Chris applied to a prestigious technical college in Indiana, the school only weighted his ACT score of 33 for 25 percent, his GPA of 3.67 65 percent, the fact that he was an Eagle Scout 5 percent and recommendations 5 percent.

On the other hand, the second type of school looks more at the whole person and gives greater weight to extracurricular activities, community service hours. An example here is that of my daughter Shireen's scholarship at Loyola University whose acceptance was influenced by the number of hours she had volunteered during high school. Another example would be The University of Evansville, which offered my son Chris a yearly $15,000 scholarship just because he was an Eagle Scout. Some schools will even remove a less than desirable ACT/SAT test score from consideration in favor of a well-rounded student.

Finally, the third type of school is looking for the next generation of leaders. In our experience, three schools of this type are Duke University, The University of Notre Dame, and Rice University. Having spoken to alumni interviewers from the schools and based upon our students' experience, it comes down to this: your student could have a perfect ACT/SAT, perfect GPA, and have 2,000 volunteer hours, but unless they've had leadership experience...forget it. That doesn't mean you have to hold office in student council or be captain of the football or volleyball team or be an Eagle Scout. Our own children headed up and organized things like the student council food drives. These also count as leadership initiatives. Schools of this type are looking for depth in your student's extracurricular activities.

The important thing to realize is that if your child waits until senior year to get active in his or her school or community, it's too late. If a college admissions committee looks at your child's application and sees that he or she has 200 volunteer hours that were all accomplished in the summer between junior and senior year, they will most certainly question your child's sincerity and authenticity.

High School Grades
[COLLEGE VIEW]

BY STEPHANIE

Freshman year can make or break you. Your first-year GPA is set in stone and greatly affects your GPA when you graduate. Even though you get all A's and B's after a low initial GPA, the numbers will barely rise. Many students I know do not take high school seriously the first two years and then shape up later, but by then it is too late. A tiny change in a GPA greatly affects the amount of scholarship money you can receive. Additionally, the overall average of grades is not all colleges look at; they receive an *entire* transcript with every class and every grade. Accordingly, admissions can tell if you have taken all "blow-off" classes to get straight A's, or if you have gotten B's in challenging courses (they prefer the second!).

Although many seniors believe themselves home free after their first semester, many are sadly disappointed when they discover that colleges require the final transcript with all the classes and grades from their last semester in order to enroll. What college would want to help out a student whose classes changed from Honors Biology to two periods of gym? Many colleges require that your GPA stay at a certain level in order to keep the scholarships you have been awarded. The bottom line is that although it is easy to procrastinate or to come down with a case of senioritis, hard work for the entire four years is a sure-fire way to help you get into your dream college and win the money that is out there because other students are slacking off when you are not.

Extracurricular Activities
[COLLEGE VIEW]

BY SHIREEN

Have you ever heard the expression, "less is more"? If we think that way in terms of school, it definitely holds true for extracurricular activities. Why do people join clubs? From what I've seen, it's one of three reasons: their parents make them, they truly care about that particular club, or the famous "it looks good on a college application." For those students who are considering joining a group just to say they are a member, here's some news: colleges are not naïve. Harvard, University of Illinois, or a smaller private school will want hard proof that you are involved. Even if you join ten clubs because you care about each of them, most likely a few of those groups will not see you as much as they need to. If you are elected to office in three clubs, despite your good intentions, you may be hurting one group in the end.

Joining groups shouldn't be about signing your name to something or just adding it on a to-do list. Hopefully it is something you are really interested it. Don't get me wrong, colleges want well-rounded students, but joining every club possible isn't exactly the way to get there.

If you see something you are interested in, you should inquire about it. Then, if you have the time and commitment to participate, feel free to try it out. Colleges like well-rounded students in the areas of sports, academics, social clubs, etc. Participation in such programs as National Honors Society, Student Ambassadors, and Math Team look great, but be involved in other areas as well. So if sports aren't your thing, maybe you can join Student Council, the newspaper, an earth club, or a multicultural club. If you truly involve yourself in more than one activity, your top-choice school may beg you to come.

Having a job is also a necessity for many high school students, which makes it more difficult to be involved in school. In that case, you just need to prioritize. Can you sacrifice five hours of work a week to be involved in the pep-band or do you need gas money? Job experience does look good to many colleges, but remember that's not all they look for.

Now you know the secrets of how colleges look at extracurricular activities. Become a well-ounded student. Sports, academics, and social clubs are all good, but one by itself doesn't stand a chance against the two or three strengths on someone else's application. The goal is not to join a million and one clubs right off the bat; start with a few to see how much time is needed to be a dedicated member. Just remember, less can most definitely be more.

Chapter 7: Degrees Offered by Various Colleges Help Narrow the Search

WHAT ARE YOU LOOKIN' AT?

"A wise son makes his father glad, but a foolish son is a grief to his mother."

PROVERBS 10:1

"College today is like a batch of French Revolutions- the students take liberties, the parents worry about fraternities, and the government insists on equalities."

ANON

BY LAYLA

There are a myriad of characteristics your child should consider when searching for the right school. Sprawling green lawns and beautiful fountains are wonderful, but happiness is more than turf-deep. This one should be obvious, but I'm always surprised to see students who head off to that very special college with no idea of a career path, only to find out that they need to transfer to another college to complete that particular major. If your children know the career path they want to pursue, this search becomes much easier. If they know their general area of interest, they can also search within those bounds. For example, if they know they will end up in engineering, mathematics, or computer science, check for schools that have all three. Typically, if a school offers engineering, it will also offer the other related fields.

If, on the other hand, they know they are drawn to the social services, such as teaching, psychology, or social work, most liberal arts colleges offer these choices, as well as many of the same general education requirements. However, if your children are like our son Michael, who was equally enamored with civil engineering, finance, and physical therapy, you'll need to help them narrow down their choice to one general career area because hardly any colleges offer all three of these majors. If they haven't been able to narrow their choices down before they begin college, they may want to choose a junior college or a state school to complete many of their general requirements while they explore their options. This way, you have not spent a great deal of money nor have they traveled far away. They still have many options open to them.

Another interesting point on this subject is that many universities will offer master's (or even doctoral) programs in one's chosen field. Some even entice prospective students by offering an automatic entrance into their master's program after successful completion of a bachelor's degree. Still others go a step further and provide a shortened master's program if one completes the bachelor's degree in the same field at that university. For example, a student could complete a four-year business degree, and then continue one more year (instead of the usual two) and complete his or her MBA (Master's in Business Administration) at that same institution. What a time-saving and money-saving opportunity!

Once your child has narrowed the list of colleges for his or her chosen major, more specific questions need to be asked. You'll want to know just how good those programs are. One very basic question is what percentage of recent graduates are employed in that field? Make sure you understand what the statistics they provide are based on. We asked one prospective college this question, and followed it up by asking how old the data was and how many students were polled. To our amazement, and the great embarrassment of the dean we were speaking to, it turned out that this college based its "90 percent employment in their field" rate on only twenty respondents to a survey sent to 200 graduates from that program.

We also like to ask people already in their chosen career field what they think of a certain college's program or if they have been impressed with the preparedness of recent graduates from this college. This can reveal a lot about a school's strengths and weaknesses. If, for example, you want to know which colleges have the best nursing schools, it would be wise to speak to a hospital administrator, a head nurse, or a doctor on the hospital staff. They will probably give you an impassioned opinion about which graduates they see as very prepared and which seem lacking in skills.

Chapter 8: College Search
FOLLOW THE FOLLOWER

"Knowledge will please your soul."

PROVERBS 2:6

"A university should be a place of
light, of liberty, and of learning."

BENJAMIN DISRAELI

Selecting the right college can be tough if you have a child who is unable to pick a major. It's nothing to freak out about, but you'll want to find out from the school how strict they are about changing majors. If your student decides to change majors and then wants to transfer, will it make a difference? Another consideration is whether your student wants a double major or a major and a minor.

In my daughter's experience, some schools would let students have a double major, for example, marketing and communications, while others would only let them have a major and a minor. Or if you had a double major you'd have to go one year longer, which in my book is unacceptable. From Shireen's standpoint, a degree in both marketing and communications gave her more flexibility and marketability. Similarly in engineering, it could be advantageous to major in computer engineering and electrical engineering. Or a double major in mechanical engineering and aerospace engineering would have a lot of potential. Look to see how flexible the college is going to be.

Public Versus Private Schools

Most people who come into my workshops are under the mistaken belief that a state school is going to be the cheapest way to go. That it is not true. When I had three children in college at the same time, and they all went to their first-choice private schools, it cost me about $4,000 more per year to send all three to private schools than to just send one of them to the University of Illinois. That's a huge difference. I am not saying that the private schools are any better; you just want to look at what financial resources are available.

In terms of private schools, you also want to give some thought to whether you are going to pick a secular private school or a faith-based school. For my first master's degree I went to a small Catholic school, University of Steubenville, and it was an awesome experience. I will treasure it forever partially because that is where I met my wife. Many non-Catholic Christian schools do not have the endowment funds and even though the environment may be great, they may not have the scholarships available. These are things you have to keep in mind. We have found that many evangelical schools also do not have the endowment funds to give your children scholarships that some of the other private schools have.

Location, Location, Location!

BY LAYLA

If being near the beach, the mountains, or a city is important to your child, then he or she should include this factor in the college search. Some students feel more comfortable in a rural or a suburban environment, whereas others crave the excitement of cities. However, considerations such as the geographic location of the college need to go beyond, "Where can I go downhill skiing on the weekends?" Remember, the main objective of a college education is just that, *an education!* In any case, encourage your child not to exclude all other schools that aren't in that original "this is what my college should look like" postcard-image. As you get a better feel of what each college is really like, your child can begin to narrow his or her search.

Clearly the location of the college your child wants to attend is something he or she will need to discuss with you. Will commuting to college be a viable option? How will your child come home to visit and how will you visit? How often you or your child expects to visit will affect his or her choice of location and distance from home. Some parents expect their college-bound student to attend a school in their home state, while others may require a three-hour radius from home to make weekend visits possible. Still others have no guidelines, and may even be comfortable with their student going to school abroad.

Yet another consideration is the educational opportunities at each particular location. Sometimes internships are offered at impressive local companies. My cousin, Karam, for example, was offered an exciting cooperative employment opportunity with Honeywell, Inc., while working on his electrical engineering degree at the University of Toronto. Since he may want to pursue employment at Honeywell after graduation, this was both an invaluable education and business connection for him. You will also want to investigate whether the staff in your college's department network with important employers in the area where you may be interested in living.

Other Factors to Consider

BY LAYLA

Our daughter Stephanie studied ocean engineering at Florida Institute of Technology. In addition to its close proximity to the ocean for first-hand experience, another attractive consideration was the fact that some professors act as consultants for the local community in the area of beach erosion, an area Stephanie ended up specializing in. Likewise, when we researched colleges in the area of business for our daughter Shireen, one of the factors we looked at closely was the business connections she could make during her college years. If she chose a school in a rural area or an out-of-state school, she would be making those connections in areas she really didn't want to live in. At Loyola University of Chicago we found a great business program with a bonus of long-time business connections all over the Chicago area. These opportunities should not be overlooked, because they do more than just provide a degree: they help build a successful student and create bridges for future employment.

This Isn't Your Parents' College Life

BY LAYLA

College was one of the most exciting and important times in my life, so naturally, I wanted to be able to give that experience and career foundation to my children. My biggest concern, however, was that it seemed impossible to fund college for four children within an age span of four and a half years! So, while the kids were still young, I made it a high priority for my husband and me to come up with a plan for their future schooling. Once a plan began to be put into place, my biggest fears were allayed.

But, as any good mom knows, that just opens up a space for the next fear to enter in! It really wasn't until we began the college tours with our first daughter that the reality of college life in the new millennium became clear. I felt just the way my parents must have felt when they sent me off to school. Their college experiences in the 1950's seemed quite archaic to me. Women's and men's colleges, dress, etiquette, and dating had all changed so much in just thirty years. And now, about thirty years after I embarked on my college career, it seemed that things had changed even more.

Some changes have been good, of course. More young men and women — from all socio-economic and racial backgrounds — are attending college than ever before! Academically, so much more is available to students. So much research and development is being conducted by college professors, and many students are given the opportunity to get first-hand glimpse of it, or even be a part of it as an upper-level or graduate student. Myriad study-abroad programs are offered — Rome, Austria, Egypt, South America! When I was in college, the few study-abroad programs were reserved for English literature or foreign language students. Now, just about anyone can find an abroad program to complement his or her major and interests. Colleges are also making more internships and co-op programs available to students, offering real-world applications and connecting students with possible future employers. Then there's the aesthetic appeal— OK, maybe only moms notice this part. I've been truly impressed at how campuses are more beautiful than ever, having invested in infrastructure and landscaping. Dorms aren't just bare-bones essential rooms anymore; they're actually pretty comfy little microcosms of life! Most are air-conditioned, upgraded, and tech-friendly.

So, what's the down side? Well, behind those beautiful ivy-covered walls, fountains, and stone pathways lie...all the characters in *Animal House*! Yes, I know, wild parties have been around for a long time. It's just that on campuses now, if you are NOT engaging in excess of every kind (we'll leave that to your imagination), you are in the minority and really have to "go against the flow." There are definitely some Christian and Catholic colleges that nurture a sane, positive atmosphere in every area of campus life, but these colleges are the exception rather than the rule. Today, most colleges with a Christian founding or Catholic name are not much different than the secular colleges, insofar as the moral practices of the students. As a parent, that reality is a bit disconcerting. We don't like to feel as if we're throwing our child (yes, I realize now fully eighteen years-old and legally an adult!) into a lion's den. So it's really important for mom, dad, and student to discern what type of college and atmosphere is desired and needed. Hopefully, all those years of upbringing have ingrained some solid beliefs and values. Honestly, some students can handle the craziness and stay on the straight path. Most, however, seem to get sucked into the roller-coaster and the hedonistic lifestyle to some extent. Maturity level, self-esteem, and experience in the real world all come into play when considering preparedness for college life. Learn, discuss, pray, talk with other parents and students about their (recent) college experiences, pray some more, and then make a decision.

Sex, Drugs, and Rock-n-roll

Conversations about college life and your expectations should occur far before the launching period; visiting colleges can provide a perfect backdrop for these discussions. College counselors always urge parents to make their expectations clear—about drinking, dating, and success in school. Be clear, but try to keep it positive. It is wise to inform your teen that if he or she demonstrates an inability to live successfully on a college campus, you will not hesitate to bring him or her home (as in the drinking binge example, above). This should not be an idle threat, but have clear examples of what would constitute dysfunctional behavior. A lifestyle of sex, drugs, and rock-n-roll may seem very appealing at this age, but you certainly do not have to fund it. Unacceptable behaviors might include alcohol abuse, drug abuse, disregard for integrity in dating relationships, or failing classes. So in those final chats before school begins, your teens should not be hearing anything new. You should reiterate your confidence in them and their ability to maintain high values as they focus on their studies. Remember, that was the primary reason for going to college, right?

Other Things to Consider When Choosing a College

✔ Size of student body

✔ Academic expectations; how will you compare with your peers?

✔ Public/state schools, private schools, and those with religious affiliation

✔ Internships, co-ops, semesters abroad

✔ Job placement percentage

How I Selected My College

BY STEPHANIE GROLEAU

After formal and informal trips to multiple schools and comparisons of financial and academic awards, I went with the school I felt most relaxed and welcomed at, Florida Institute of Technology. I loved the palm trees scattered throughout the campus, friendly students walking around, the ocean a couple miles east, and professors who surfed during their lunch breaks. Other schools had offered me promising scholarships, but I didn't feel the same connection to the professors and I didn't have the same confidence in their overall program. A small amount of school loans was worth the perfect fit.

How I Selected My College

BY SHIREEN GROLEAU

Because my majors were not too specialized, I had a lot of leeway in what university I would attend. To give me a head start, my mother signed me up for about five school tours the summer after my sophomore year. I was excited. Knowing that these schools already had my majors, I could go straight to the important questions:

1. How good are your sports teams?

2. Do you have sororities and fraternities?

3.   Is there a student council?

4.   What kind of information about me is sent home to my parents?

Yes, I wanted to attend a good school. But obviously although some of the other things I was concerned with seemed like a big deal to me at the time, my parents had more important concerns.

Thank God my father was there to keep some of my nonsense straightened out. I also had to consider the importance of school location and distance from home. Once I started looking more seriously, it became apparent that I was very attracted to city schools...not that far from home. I decided on Loyola University in Chicago for a number of reasons:

1.   It had great programs for my areas of study.

2.   I was more than excited to explore the best city in America.

3.   They offered me a great academic scholarship.

4.   I could really envision myself getting involved on campus.

Loyola was not the absolute perfect fit for me, but I don't think any school would have been 100 percent. I'm certainly glad I went there, and I think it turned out well.

How I Selected My College

BY MICHAEL GROLEAU

I selected my college based on many reasons. I had visited all seven colleges where I applied, and found that they each had their own particular environments; city, outskirts of town, middle of nowhere, etc. As I didn't really enjoy the city life, I narrowed the choice down to campuses that were more self-sufficient. This left the University of Dayton and Florida Institute of Technology. My sister was currently attending the latter school. While this did weigh in its favor, I felt that FIT would put a lot more pressure on "extracurricular" activities. (Translation: I did not want to be pressured into drinking and partying when that was counter to the direction I wanted my life to take.)

The University of Dayton was a Catholic Marianist school. I only understood the Catholic part, but that was enough for me. On top of giving me around $25,000 per year in scholarships and grants to attend, there was a certain "feeling" on campus. I realize that is a vague term, but that's what it was. I could literally feel the community on campus and feel welcomed. And no, I'm not making that up because almost every single person that attends UD says the same thing. Amazing. In addition to all of that, UD had an excellent engineering program. All of these factors put together are why I chose UD to be my home and place of learning for the next four years of my life.

How I Selected My College

BY CHRIS GROLEAU

I visited many colleges on my search. Some I visited with my brother or sister when they were looking for the right college (they are both engineering majors), and some I visited later when it was time for me to choose a college. This was actually the easiest part of the college experience for me, on account of how I felt about all the colleges I visited except for one. I'm a big believer in following and listening to your gut instinct, and almost every college I went to simply felt wrong. I could call it the atmosphere, the energy, or something else, but I simply knew I did not want to spend any more time at those schools. When I visited the University of Dayton with my brother Michael, I could have told you five minutes later this was the place for me. Over a year has passed and I couldn't be happier with my choice.

Chapter 9: Making the Most of Campus Visits

HOLY JEANS, APATHY AND DUMB QUESTIONS

"Seek counsel from every wise man, and do not think lightly of any advice that can be useful."

TOBIT 4:18

"He who is ashamed of asking is ashamed of learning."

DANISH PROVERB

Most kids go to a college campus and interview with the admissions counselors saying, "Pick me! Please pick me!" But if you're going to spend $30,000 to $40,000 a year or more, shouldn't you be interviewing them? You have just as much right to grill them as they have to grill a potential student. So developing the right questions is crucial.

When my daughter and I went to visit the University, I asked the dean of the business college the placement percentage for marketing students. Basically that means what percentage of students in marketing get a job in marketing. Most people don't even ask that. Instead they'll ask what percentage of students get a job when they graduate. Up until the past couple years, many schools would say between 80 and 90 percent and you'd think, "Well, that sounds pretty good." So you want to take it the next step further and ask, what percentage of students in your child's major are getting a job in that field?

The dean responded to my question that 90 percent of marketing students were getting a job in marketing when they graduated. And then I threw the curveball at him. I said, "Well, Dean, that's great, but what's the sampling size?" and there was dead silence. He had no idea and told me he would get back to me with that information. I told him I was happy to wait since we had driven all that way.

So we waited while he frantically searched through all of his files. Finally, he had an answer: "Well, Mr. Groleau, we had 200 students who graduated with a marketing degree, and we sent out 200 questionnaires; 20 questionnaires came back and 18 got a job in marketing." Well, I could do the math, and figured that 18/20 is 90 percent hence 90 percent of their marketing students got a job in marketing when they graduated.

"Where are the other 180 students?" I asked. He said he didn't know. At this point I got a little hot under the collar. "You want me to spend $40,000 a year and the best you can give me is a 10 percent response rate from three-year-old data?" I asked incredulously. At this point my lovely daughter Shireen started sliding in her seat, hoping she could kind of just whisk herself away. But you need to understand that colleges will tell you what they think you want to hear.

So, when selecting a college, I suggest that you have at least two visits. The first visit is to see the school. You might have the deer-in-the-headlights look and you will probably miss some key information. Or even worse, you'll drink that particular college's "Kool-Aid" and fall in love and not want to look any further. On the second visit, as much as possible, I strongly encourage you and your student to arrange an overnight class-shadow. It will give you the opportunity to stay in a dorm, see what the students are like, and the next day go to a class and see what the professors are like. Now, one of the things you want to do is make sure your student is staying with an upper classman, preferably someone in his or her major. Why? Because freshman don't know anything, sophomores know little or next to nothing, and the admissions counselors are only going to tell you what they want you to hear. So, the best source of information to find out what it's like with financial aid, getting jobs on campus, dealing with professors, internships, and especially job placement is to ask an upperclassman in your student's intended major.

Making the Most of Your College Visit

Most parents spend more time planning their vacations than their children's college visits. Why is this? Perhaps they have not thought about it, or perhaps they assume that the colleges will tell you everything you need to know. My experience has shown me that this is far from the truth. The good news is that with a little forethought and planning, your campus visits can be memorable, fun, and productive.

There are four types of college visits you can take. The first is a virtual tour. This involves going to the school's website or to sites that aggregate college virtual tours such as www.campustours.com. I would recommend these only if you are absolutely unable to visit a school, or as a way of getting first acquainted with a school before you go there in person. (Never allow your child to attend a college you haven't visited in person.)

If you have to do a virtual tour, be sure to find alternate ways to get your questions answered: blogs, admission chat rooms, alumni, college reps, Google, Collegeboard, Facebook, etc. Next, informal or "drive-by" tours are great when you are in the early stages of your college search. These are often done in the summer and/or during spring break. Little planning is required and these are less structured. Local colleges are a good place to start, and if you are organized you can probably visit three to four colleges in a day.

During the informal visits, you can take advantage of campus tours. Do call ahead. Try to arrange a meeting with an admissions counselor and the head of the department your child wishes to enter. Also take advantage of any information sessions offered. Finally, don't forget to eat in the student union, walk around, and check out as many facilities as possible. (We once had a student who was a vegetarian and decided not to attend the school of her dreams when she saw the salad bar because she thought it looked like a "train wreck"!)

The third type of tour is the formal tour. This will give you a lot of information. In my experience, the first couple of formal visits helped my kids and me move from "the deer in the headlights" first-time syndrome to a more conscious, strategic visit. Then we shifted to informal visits where we zeroed in on the specific people and topics we wanted to cover. For most campuses the formal tours will last up to three hours, so don't expect to get more than two schools in per day.

The best times to do formal tours are when school is in session. Remember to call ahead to secure a space. For instance, Marquette is booked more than three months ahead, especially during peak times.

The fourth and final tour is the overnight/class-shadow tour. Here students get to participate first hand in campus activities. They live on campus for a night, eat campus food, and see what students do in their spare time. This allows them to experience the many social aspects of the school. They also get to attend classes, which is very important. The instructor is usually the reason a student has a favorite class—or a least favorite class. So getting to connect to the professors is a crucial variable in making a decision. It could be the difference between your child surviving or thriving in college.

I would suggest that for your top two or three schools you should visit a second time, and as much as possible that second visit should be an overnight/class-shadow tour.

Typically with my children we did a formal tour for a couple schools. When we narrowed down our school list we went back for an informal tour but made sure we got in contact with the specific people—professors, heads of departments, etc. — we wanted to see. This way we had meetings in private where we could drill down further and get more specific answers to our most pressing questions.

Times to Visit

During the week Mondays through Thursdays are ideal. High school days off are not always college days off. Additionally, spring break and early summer as well as late summer and early September before senior year are good times. Fall through Winter and sometimes early Spring are great for revisits.

Avoid Thanksgiving weekend, Christmas week, winter and spring breaks, and summer when school is *not* in session. Also, avoid visiting when classes are not meeting such as during: reading period, exam weeks, and Saturdays and Sundays. Also check when the admissions office is closed to visitors.

Interviewing the Interviewer
[COLLEGE VIEW]

BY SHIREEN

College visits and interviews are essential elements in finding the right school. I have always found that while visiting, meeting with other perspective students, and touring the campus were the most entertaining, the interviews, although a few steps away from being called fun, were definitely beneficial.

The most important thing to remember is to come prepared. This ranges from the way you present yourself, to what you know about the school, to the questions you want to ask. Just as the college is interviewing you, you are interviewing the college.

Unfortunately, I found this out the hard way. It was the summer after my sophomore year of high school and my mother and I decided to visit one of the surrounding private universities. I was forced to get out of my jeans before we left so I threw on some khakis and a polo as we set off on our drive. My mom had printed off some information about the school and asked me to read it on the way there. But, as I had gotten up early, I found it much more important to catch some extra sleep.

We arrived at the school and marched up proudly to the admissions office for our interview. I couldn't wait to do a little bragging about my good grades and high volume of school activities. But, to my disappointment, there was little talk about my accomplishments. The admissions counselor pulled out a fat book about the school and asked, "So, what do you know about the Jesuit tradition?" Jesuit, Jesuit, Jesuit, was racing through my mind. Well, I knew they are a Catholic order. So that's what I said, "I know they are a Catholic order." Nice move. She gave me a smile, and moved on. As our interview progressed, she continued asking me questions, none of which I knew the answers to. Finally, toward the end of the interview, her final question was, "Now, do you have any questions?" Good thinking, Shireen. I knew I should have done *something*.

"Uh, no. Thank you, though." Needless to say I left that meeting feeling quite bewildered and very foolish.

Now, some may call that a failure of a meeting, but I call that a learning experience. From then on I dressed my best, researched the school beforehand, and definitely came up with my own set of questions. Why visit a school if you have no intention of finding anything out about it? First impressions mean a lot to schools, so while they're discovering who you are, make sure you do just as good a job of interviewing them.

Summing it Up

✔ Do your research.

✔ Call ahead or visit the campus website to find out tour dates, campus or preview days and times, and secure a space.

✔ Contact academic offices separately to arrange time with faculty or visit a classroom.

✔ Prepare a list of questions to bring with you.

✔ Map out your trip.

ANOTHER CIRCLE TO FILL IN

"The LORD tests the good and the bad."

PSALM 11:5

"I'm glad I did it, partly because it was worth it, but mostly because I shall never have to do it again."

MARK TWAIN

Aptitude Testing, Interest Exams, and Personality Inventories

BY LAYLA GROLEAU

Know Thyself

Aptitude testing basically tests what we are good at. It assesses one's ability in several key areas such as mathematical, reading, writing, or even mechanical areas. Standardized tests such as the ACT and SAT college placement exams are good examples of well-accepted exams which identify strengths and relative weaknesses. The ACT (American College Test) tests mathematics, reading comprehension, knowledge of grammatical usage in language, writing ability, and science understanding. The SAT (Scholastic Achievement Test) tests in two general areas: verbal and mathematical. Verbal assessment includes reading comprehension and vocabulary. Both types of exams have recently added a writing component. The purpose of these tests is to predict academic success in college, and they do a fairly good job of that, aside from lowered scores due to language barriers and "test stress." They can also be used to identify broad strengths and weaknesses. But clearly, there are many areas of strength that these tests do not address.

There are several different tools available to help us determine our strengths. If we refer to Howard Gardner's seven areas of intelligence, we can look at the total person. Gardner's use of the term intelligence more broadly describes the ways human beings find to become useful in society. He differentiates these "intelligences" into the following areas: 1) mathematical/logical, 2) verbal-speaking, reading, and writing, 3) spatial, 4) intrapersonal—introspective, reflective, 5) interpersonal—ability to relate well with others, 6) musical, and 7) bodily-kinesthetic.

Another way to look at the total person is to determine learning style. Learning styles are simply different approaches or ways of learning. The three types of learning styles are visual, auditory, and kinesthetic.

It is very interesting to determine your own strongest learning styles or intelligences. There are myriad surveys for multiple intelligences and learning styles online. Simply search *multiple intelligence test* or *learning style test*.

In order to round out our evaluation as a whole person, interest and personality inventories help answer the questions about what we love doing and what is important to us. Typical questions might be, "Do you enjoy tinkering with electronic equipment?" or "Do you enjoy sitting for an hour doing paperwork?" Interest inventories are sometimes offered to students by their high schools along with corresponding career groups that match one's responses.

Personality inventories are a bit more complex. Many psychologists have branched out from Carl Jung's theories to produce different personality profiles based on beliefs and behaviors. Perhaps the most commonly used is the Myers-Briggs Personality Profile. A simple online search will also produce several surveys you can take. You may be asked if you prefer socializing or being alone, for example. The results of many of these surveys also suggest career groups suited to each personality type.

All of these surveys are helpful indicators, but obviously no single test can give a comprehensive analysis. [SC1] Some time spent getting to know oneself in a way that provides some concrete results as to areas of strength will be invaluable in finding one's career path. Remember, even Socrates admonished us, "Know thyself."

College View

BY STEPHANIE

The ACT and SAT are not normal exams. They are based on what you should have already learned in school, so there is little "real" studying to do. The secret is *practice*. There are many study books available in your local library and bookstores which are very helpful. If you are well-disciplined and really take the time to prepare on your own, these can be great tools. Most high school kids, however, do not have the desire or the self-initiative to put in the required effort to make a difference.

Another helpful tool is the opportunity to take an ACT or SAT preparatory class. Often high schools, junior colleges, and private organizations offer these classes. Compare the price, the schedule that best meshes with your own, and most importantly, the format of the class. Some classes simply go over test-prep booklets with you, then have you take practice tests. Other classes actually customize to the needs of the students, providing re-teaching for areas where students scored poorly on their practice tests.

Because of the lack of structure in my particular class, I learned more at home studying on my own than at the actual class. As I said before, you should already know most of what will be on the test, but once you take your first practice test, go back and look at the types of problems you missed. Did you have difficulty with prepositions, analyzing poetry, or trigonometry? If you go to a top-quality prep class, they will give you a large book filled with practice tests, answer keys, explanations, and reviews. Go through it, studying only the things you have had trouble with. The most important thing is to take each practice test as if it counted. Do one subject at a time, using a timer, with no cheating and no distractions; this way you can figure out how to manage your time. Even if you know every answer, when time runs out, that test is over. When the Big Day is closer, try to focus on the sections of the test that are most troublesome, whether it be English, math, or science.

Another important thing to consider is which test is best for you, the ACT or SAT? It is very important to find out which tests your chosen colleges require. Many schools have a definite preference, and you'll need to concentrate on preparing for that specific test. Some schools, though, accept both or either, taking the highest score of any of the tests you have taken. If this is the case with your preferred colleges, concentrate on getting higher scores on whichever test you are better at. In my case, I happened to do very well on the ACT, but when I took a practice SAT, the equivalent score was quite a bit lower than my ACT score. Had I known that one of the East-coast schools I applied to only accepted the SAT score, I certainly would have prepared as hard for that test as I did for the ACT.

ACT Prep

BY JOHN

In studying for the ACT it is worth spending the money for a good prep class. Most high schools offer large-scale nationally known programs. While they tend to be the least expensive, I've generally found you get what you've paid for.

There are four crucial components that affect your ACT score: (1) subject knowledge, (2) time management skills, (3) test-taking strategies, and (4) test anxiety. A good ACT or SAT prep class will focus on subject knowledge, time management skills, and test-taking strategies. What we've found, especially for our brighter students, is that they know everything on the test. The question is whether they have enough time to get all of the answers down. Time management skills are crucial. Students tend to go through question 1, question 2, hit question 3 and realize, "That's a toughie," focus on that question until they get it, move on to question 4, 5, 6, 7, run into question 8, another toughie, and get stuck on that until completing it. Instead, go through 1,2, and if you don't know 3, skip it, move on to 4, 5, 6, 7 skip 8 and any other tough questions you can't immediately answer. Finish that portion of the test and then come back to the questions you got stuck on. The more difficult standardized test component to deal with is test anxiety. I am not aware of any ACT/SAT prep classes that deal with this. Most of the time when you think of test anxiety, you are thinking absolute brain lockdown and going blank like some alien just sucked out your intelligence. While this may happen, the more prevalent form is milder. One resource we've used successfully is Dr. Alfred Frost III out of Buffalo, New York, who has done numerous studies on test anxiety and found that just a little bit of adrenaline in the system dramatically inhibits memory recall. I have bought dozens of his "Steady State" CDs, which we have handed out to our students to help them practice relaxation.

Dr. Frost uses relaxation and visualization techniques, similar to what the Olympic athletes use. I used this technique when I recently completed my second master's degree, and it really saved my bacon to pass that final exam. My son Michael also used Dr. Frost's CD during his junior year when he was struggling with two of his killer engineering classes. Michael has always been a good test taker but was feeling overwhelmed that year. He actually had blanked out on a couple of exams, which is totally uncharacteristic for him. After listening and putting the techniques into practice, Michael regained his normal "karma" and was back in the groove again.

ACT/SAT and the Bottom Line

Every school looks at admissions differently with regard to merit aid, but in general they first review the ACT or SAT scores. Most schools do not care which you take, although elite schools will require SAT II, which is the subject SAT test. In general, though, the benchmark for most schools to give out merit aid based upon ACT score requires a score of 25. For example in one of the nearby small private colleges here in Illinois, if you have an ACT of 25 they will give you $5,000 a year, 27 $2,000 more, 29 another $2,000 more.

At Loyola, where one of our daughters attended college, the beginning benchmark to start giving merit aid for an ACT seemed to be a 27 or a 28. The top score ACT score I have seen (33) at that particular school netted about $15,000 per year. The nice thing about this money is that the scholarships the schools will give you are renewed every year as long as you maintain your GPA in school. Once you get above a 34, however, then you might start getting free tuition, and in some cases a complete full ride. It is not as common as it used to be, but there are still schools out there as long as you are willing to look for them.

Regarding ACT/SAT scores, most schools will allow you to take it three times, and use the best score out of three. Some schools will actually "superscore" and take the best components of each of the tests you've taken. With the ACTs you can decide which score you want to send to the school, while the SATs send all of your scores out. If you are wondering which test to take, the ACT or SAT, the ACT is an achievement test, while the SAT is an aptitude test. They're different in structure and in scoring, such as whether you get penalized for wrong answers. So I suggest you have your child study for whichever test he or she has a better chance of obtaining a high score on.

One of the keys to look at merit aid for ACT scores is to find the schools that will pay your child to go there. In particular, if you are trying to see if your child can receive any scholarships based on ACT scores, look for schools where your child's ACT score is above the average. When my daughter, Stephanie, decided to go into engineering, and she was looking to apply to MIT, she had a phenomenal ACT score of 34. Well, most kids who go to MIT have an ACT score of 34 or higher, and as a matter of fact I have yet to work with a student who got into MIT with a score less than 35. So basically if your child's ACT score falls within the school's average, your child is essentially a small fish swimming in a big pond. If your child's score is above the average, then they are a big fish swimming in a small pond. The big fish usually get the merit aid.

Chapter 11: Applications and Essays
"STRUTTIN' YOUR STUFF"

"For I myself shall give you a wisdom in speaking that all your adversaries will be powerless to resist."

LUKE 21:15

"One of a kind isn't much of a poker hand, but it's a pretty good description of a real leader."

ANON

BY SHIREEN

A college admissions counselor not only has the job of determining if a student applicant meets the entrance requirements for the college/university he or she represents, but also of evaluating whether a student applicant will "fit" and feel comfortable on campus.

With this in mind, it is important you take every opportunity to provide the admissions counselor with information that will assist in determining who you really are. Your application, transcript, letters of recommendation, and resume are certainly important documents that demonstrate your academic, extracurricular, leadership, and volunteer involvement. But you are much more than what the paperwork reveals. You are unique. An admissions counselor recognizes this and wants to know as much as possible about just who you are. It is the personal essay that gives you the opportunity to reveal aspects of your life that are not fully described in any "paperwork" you submit. Do not consider the personal essay as optional; you will miss an important opportunity that could cost you admission into a college or university of your dreams.

Because the personal essay is unstructured (free-style writing), most students become overwhelmed trying to guess what an admissions counselor wants to hear. *Relax!* This essay will be in narrative form; it will be a story from start to finish. The essay does not have to be long. It should just be a good story with a strong voice. Use detail to give the story depth. It can be written in first person.

Choose a topic you feel strongly about (but avoid controversial, offensive, or outrageous topics which could bring doubt about your character to the reader). Tell about the experience step by step: Tell what happened, tell why this experience had such an impact on you, and what you learned from it. Explain how this experience made you a better person or just how it changed your thoughts or beliefs from one perspective to another.

Tell the truth. Be yourself. Be authentic and let your true character come through. To test your authenticity, give the essay to a person who knows you well. Ask them to read it. They should be able to tell that it was *you* who wrote this essay because no one else could have told it the way you did!

Write (and rewrite) the story as if you are holding a conversation with the reader. The essay should give the reader an inside view of how you are unique, what you are passionate about, how you have grown and matured over the years, what makes you "tick." Let others read your story and give input—but remember, this is YOUR story. You be the judge. Do not make changes if you believe it changes your story to the point where it no longer is a true reflection of you. However, pay close attention if punctuation, spelling, or other mechanical errors are pointed out.

As the admissions counselor reads your essay, he or she is looking for clues as to your interests, values, personality— looking for clues that you will be very happy and successful on this particular college campus (thrive vs survive).

Although none of us likes extra work, try to look at this as a "golden opportunity" to demonstrate what a unique person you are. You have a captive audience—use it to your advantage!

College Application Essay:
THE CHEAT SHEET

Impression

The purpose of the college application essay is to leave the admissions counselors with a great impression of who you are. They read the essay to learn something about you that cannot be found elsewhere. *Be unique. Be yourself.* Leave them with an understanding of:

- ✔ Your goals

- ✔ Important life experiences

- ✔ Nonacademic accomplishments

- ✔ What makes you different from every other 17-year-old applicant

Topics

Although many colleges will give you essay choices, many also have the option of submitting a "personal essay." This is very open-ended, but should not be taken lightly. The Common Application (good for more than 400 schools) has six choices for essays. Listed below are a few that would also be great for the personal essay.

✔ Evaluate a significant experience, achievement, risk, or ethical dilemma you've faced and its impact on you. (Chance to demonstrate introspection, self-awareness, and self-analysis.)

✔ Discuss an issue of personal, local, national, or international concern and its importance to you. (*Not* meant for ranting about a topic. Show your character and passion.)

✔ Indicate a person who has had a significant influence on you and describe that influence. (Discuss, show depth, and analyze. Be careful who you choose; they probably see a lot of Mom and Dad.)

✔ Given your personal background, describe an experience that illustrates what you would bring to the diversity in a college community, or an encounter that demonstrated the importance of diversity to you. (Not necessarily about race, although it could be.)

✔ Describe a character in fiction, a historical figure, or a creative work (as in art, music, science, etc.) that has had an influence on you, and explain that influence. (What makes it powerful or influential?)

✔ Topic of your choice. (This *does not* mean submitting a random essay you wrote for a class. Although it may show that you are a good writer, this is *not* what colleges are looking for.)

Must Dos

✔ Answer the question fully. If there are many parts to the question, address each part fully.

✔ Write about something different than what's included elsewhere, i.e. don't write about grades. If you have written or answer a short essay question about your favorite club, don't write about that same club for another question.

✔ Be honest.

✔ Introductions and conclusions are very important, considering your essay is probably only looked at for one to two minutes, the beginning and end need to stand out. Don't merely summarize the rest of the essay. Draw the reader in, be interesting, and leave them with a great impression.

✔ Include why you are right for them *and* why they are right for you. A balance of these is key. Colleges have thousands of applicants all claiming they are applying to the perfect school. What specifically makes them unlike any other? And what will you bring to enhance the campus?

Don'ts

✔ Be too controversial.

✔ Be sarcastic. A touch of humor is the most that should be included, as this does not carry as well when it is written. (And don't assume everyone thinks you're funny).

✔ Put down others. It's okay to disagree and recognize differences in others. It is not okay to come across as greater-than-thou.

✔ Be negative.

✔ Be generic. Instead, bring light to you and your uniqueness.

✔ Go over requested word counts. If the college asks for 300 words, do not give them 301!

Grammar and Style Are Very Important!

✔ Avoid contractions in formal essays.

✔ Spell out numbers

✔ Transition! This is one of the most common mistakes. You must use transitions for the beginning and end of paragraphs, and even in between sentences. Especially when many colleges give multi-part essay questions, transitioning to make your essay make sense is crucial.

✔ Vary the word structure and sentence structure. There is nothing worse than reading an essay where every sentence starts with "I am…." or the same three adjectives are repeated fifteen times.

✔ It is very obvious when you use a thesaurus. *Simple words are better than complicated words that don't fit well.*

✔ Do not use the word *"you."* On the rare occasion that you are asking the reader a question, this is acceptable. But using the second person is simply not good writing. *Example of what not to do: If you try your hardest, you will achieve everything you want.* These are personal essays. Speak only for yourself. *I now know that by giving my all, I will truly be able to achieve my dreams.*

✔ Watch your tone: Are you being negative? Boastful? How do you want to portray yourself?

✔ Style is important, but content is more important. Do not get lost speaking in metaphor.

Essay Samples

Following are six essays for you to use as models for what to do and what not to do.

GOOD

Note: Although I am not sure what the question is, the following is a very good essay.

UIC-honors

Because of this, it has been an additional challenge to balance both swimming and school. Yet, in my defiance of my parents' wishes, I made sure I excelled at school and still balanced time for swimming and fun. Thus, I have learned to prioritize my work and get ahead of things. I plan ahead and do my homework and projects well before they are due so I am not rushed during my hectic week to finish them. I have gained so much from the team. I have learned what teamwork really means. Not coming to practice is not an option. I go to every practice not only because I want to, but also because the team needs me. As co-captain of forty-five girls, I have learned the value of good leadership. I can now effectively organize a group and am not afraid to speak up.

My initial motivation to join the team out of rebelliousness against my parents turned into a gradual confidence upsurge and relentless work ethic. This work ethic will no doubt stand me in good stead as I pursue my unwavering goal to practice medicine. Though it will be a rigorous journey, the skills I have learned from the team will continue to yield success through my journey of studying chemistry at UIC.

Comment: This is exactly what colleges are looking for. The student illustrates how her everyday routine and activities have shaped who she is, her leadership skills, and how she is able to accomplish everything on her plate. She clearly demonstrates her growth, and summarizes by applying these lessons to who she will become in college. Not only is the substance of the essay appropriate, but it is also very well written and transitioned. She leaves that admissions staff with a clear picture of who she is and how she will contribute to her future college.

GOOD

If you had the opportunity to have a conversation with an important figure, either contemporary of historical, whom would you choose? Why?

Many scientists have made enormous contributions to their fields, but none have had to work on such a controversial project with as much moral quandary as J. Robert Oppenheimer. Director of the Manhattan Project, commissioned with creating the first nuclear weapons, Oppenheimer was not only a genius but a charismatic personality capable of effectively leading a group. As I aspire to be a physicist myself, it should come as no surprise that I look up to the individual some call the founder of modern theoretical physics in the United States. But the reason I would choose to have a conversation with him specifically is that he had to live the rest of his life, due to the nature of his accomplishments, with the moral responsibilities of a scientist who helped bring the world into the nuclear age. After being embarrassingly removed from his public office, he spent the rest of his life very troubled and ashamed at the abuse of what his hands had created. It would be interesting to talk with him, to see how he feels about his contributions to science and their effects, and whether he has any regrets. Finally, I would like to find out what he feels like is the ultimate goal for a scientist, when one knows it has gone too far, and what he thinks is a scientist's responsibility to the rest of the world.

Comment: This is a phenomenal response. I chose to showcase this essay portion because this student uses his topic to stand out. College admissions counselors read countless essays on Mom and Dad's heroism, on students who struggle to make the team or the winning shot, and on the over-popular "who I admire" question. It is important to remember that when topics such as those are given to write about, students really need to be unique. This student chose to write about someone most of his peers have probably never heard of. This was an excellent choice because it demonstrates that this student is not only familiar with those who have made significant contributions to his field, but also has the ability to think deeply about others' impact on the world.

BAD - *I'm pretty sure this is a personal statement.*

Blonde is on the TV as the party girl who gets around, or the air head that knows nothing. So when people first meet me their immediate impression is just that; that I am some air head, and really naïve girl. Well I am just going to put it out there that, I am far from an air head, and most of the people that are described as blonde are fake blondes so stop grouping me with them. I take the hardest classes and excel in them. I am involved in clubs like Key Club, Student Council, and church youth organizations. I take on roles of leadership in every aspect of my life, from church to Eventing with my horse. I love to compete and love to debate. I am constantly making lists and scheduling when I have to do things. Put me in charge of something I care about and I am unstoppable. Why then are people constantly saying things like "wait you are in charge of that" or "honey are you sure you are in my class?" Blonde like all labels gives an inaccurate picture of who I am and what I can do with my life. So as I continue to disprove the stereotype of dizzy blondes, I can agree with just one: in my experience, blondes do have more fun.

Comment: If you are on the fence of getting into a college and want to be rejected, send an essay like this. The topic, tone, and message of this essay are all completely inadvisable. This student spent her entire essay writing about how she has been discriminated against as a blonde but overcame the stereotype. Not only is this ridiculous because blonde stereotypes are more of a cliché and not readily believed, but also she victimizes herself and then seems to show off about her accomplishments. This is not what colleges are looking for. If one were to have experienced and overcome actual discrimination, that would be an appropriate topic. To exaggerate a stereotype is not. Keep in mind that most humor found in college application essays is not actually that humorous to anyone but the writer.

BAD - Personal statement.

I attended Batavia Senior High School and I consider myself a very dependable and organized person. The way I express these characteristics would be through my everyday school work and activities. When it comes to school I get the work done when it needs to be done that way I have time for my other hobbies like football and helping the community. Other extra curricular activities I have done are track for three years and this year was my first year in wrestling and when the season was over I was given the award for most improved. When it comes to education I have been on the honor roll all three years and continually push myself to the fullest to achieve that goal. Being in a sport really gives me the team aspect when it comes to working with other people. I feel I work well with others. If I am given a task to complete, I will put all my effort into that project to have the best outcome. I am a very active person whether it's doing home work, sports, or helping the neighboring child city school, Mooseheart.

Comment: This is another great example of what not to do for an essay. It's boring and uninspired. A personal statement allows the student to tell a story and intrigue the reader. It should paint a vivid picture of who the student is, and leave the reader feeling honored to be able have such a personal look into someone else's experience. This is literally taking a resume and putting it into sentence form instead of bullet points. The purpose of the essay is to illustrate a side that has not yet been seen in the application. The personal statement should NOT be a page full of every personal detail about you. Instead, it should take one or two details of your life, and make them extremely personal to you and the reader.

BAD

Your life is a journey with endless lessons; it's how you use your lessons that make your life. Life always goes by so quickly. Where does it go? Have you learned anything? Only being seventeen years old I can say I've learned so much already just by the moments I've had in it. You know a moment's special when it leaves an imprint on your heart, whether it is a vacation or something you accomplished in sports, it won't leave you because it had some sort of impact on you.

Comment: A big mistake many students make is getting lost in the wording of their writing. This introduction I believe was intended to sound eloquent and inquisitive. Instead, it's uninformative and filled with fluff. There are a few specific problems with this introduction. First, "You" should not be used in formal essays, period. Second, the point of the introduction is to introduce the essay to the reader. This introduction does not give the reader any idea of what the real subject of the essay will be. This writer could have easily explained what kind of inspiring experience she had, and how she knows she will always be impacted by it. Instead, she spent a paragraph explaining what a significant experience is. If you have something inspiring and thoughtful to say, then say it, and move on to the substance.

GOOD - Share an experience that made a lasting impact on you.

Intro: It was a serene, snow-touched February night when a bus departed South Elgin High School. This bus was the steed of forty high-school students who were embarking upon a "Pay It Forward Tour". This service trip consisted of a handful of students piling into a bus and traveling around the Midwest to different service projects, led by a few college guides. I had joined this tour with parochial dreams of changing the world, feeding the poor, inspiring broken hearts, and truly making a difference in this world. I was only sixteen years old at the beginning of this trip, and I think it is certainly fair to say that many people in this world have at one point in time had extreme goals or dreams of impacting the world. I was truly blessed with the encounters and experiences of "paying it forward".

Conclusion: I realized at that point, that what I leave behind in this world is not necessarily embedded in my biggest accomplishments or even in acknowledgement, but rather it is woven into the lives of others. Victory is inspiring because he reflects the potential we all share to change our own lives for the better, as well as our ability to impact the world. Perhaps he is not ending world hunger or finding the cure to cancer, and I might not either. I realized that true leadership, as well as true charity, is not about the recognition, but the impact. I embarked on this tour with a mindset of changing the world and helping others, but the truth is that he was there to help me just as much as I was there to help him. - Justin Kochanski

Comment: This is one of the best essays I have edited. The student has an amazing introduction and conclusion. Just by reading these two paragraphs the reader sees how he grew as a person and what life lessons he will take with him. His writing is descriptive, thought-provoking, and generally inspiring. He clearly sums up his experience and what he learned in a mature and well-written manner.

Chapter 12: The EFC or

EXTREMELY SCREWED-UP CALCULATION

"Such men change the night into day; where there is darkness they talk of approaching light."

JOB 17:12

"There are lies, damn lies, and then there are statistics."

BENJAMIN DISRAELI

I remember when I was working with my daughter Stephanie when she was first interested in marine biology, but before she went to Career Vision. One of the schools we looked at was the University of Miami, which is an awesome school. I did all the calculations and figured out that because I could lower our expected family contribution (EFC), she would be able to go to there. Although the tuition at the time was around $37,000 per year, it would only cost us about $7,000 to $8,000.

I said excitedly to my wife, "Honey, I think Stephanie will be able to go to University of Miami, and it's only going to cost us about $7,000-$8,000 a year!" She looked at me and said, "I don't believe you." Can you believe it? The love of my life, my partner, my best friend, accusing me of a falsehood. Well, Layla spent her entire summer vacation from teaching proving me wrong. She was doing all the research, reading all the books, and then by the end of the summer she said four words that every husband would like to hear: "Honey, you were right."

In addition to Stephanie's academic qualifications, part of what lowered the cost for The University of Miami was our EFC.

One of the key terms in financial aid is Expected Family Contribution or EFC. Personally I think we should call it "extremely screwed-up calculation," and here is why. The EFC is calculated using a very complicated formula. But what it comes down to is *what the government says you can afford to pay* before you qualify for need-based aid. As a reminder, need-based aid is made up of student loans, work study, and grants. The technical term for grants is "gift aid."

This is money that you don't have to pay back. Loans are known as called "self help." This sounds friendly, but you have to pay it back and they can garnish your or your child's wages if you DON'T pay the monies back.

EFC is affected by parents' income and assets, student's income and assets, age of the parents, how many children they have, age of the children, and how far apart in age they are. To give you an idea of how it works in my area, the average family EFC is $35,000. This means that unless your child's college costs more than $35,000 a year you don't get any need-based aid other than Federal Student Loans. So you have to come up with the first $35,000 and the school will come up with the rest — in theory.

So, for example, say you sent your child to the University of Illinois where the cost the cost of attendance is $30,000 per year. With an EFC of $35,000, you would not get anything. If on the other hand your child were to go to the University of Chicago, which is something like $65,000, you would pay $35,000 and the school would come up with the rest.

Note that there is an adjustment for EFC each year for inflation. When I was first working with Stephanie planning for her college in 2003, I was able to use several college-planning loopholes for my business, allowing me to reduce my adjusted gross income to about $100,000. That year my EFC was approximately $7,600. In 2011, everything remaining the same, my EFC would be $32,000. So even if my income had not changed, EFC went up almost five-fold!

The bottom line, in my opinion, is that the system is broken. This is totally unfair and beyond what the average family can afford to pay for college. What this means for families who have children in college is that because the EFC is increasing every year, the amount of need-based aid will decrease each year even if your assets stay the same.

Another important point is that the EFC is a "per-family number." At the time I had three children in college at the same time, my EFC was $36,000. So with my three children in school, the EFC got split three ways, distributing the amount at $12,000 per child.

This can have a huge impact on reducing your college expenses **provided you find the schools that give you great financial aid packages**. If your child's EFC is $18,000 and she applies to the University of Illinois, based on our experience with families you will still have to write a check for $30,000 to go to U of I. Just because you qualify for $18,000 in financial aid doesn't mean they are going to give it to you. Other schools known as "need-blind schools" will give you the remaining financial aid with a mixture of grants, loans, and work study. The vast majority of these schools, however, are private schools. Understanding this concept is what enabled us to send three of our children to private schools at the same time for roughly only three or four thousand dollars more per year than it would have cost to send one of them to a state school. It doesn't mean necessarily that the private schools provide a better education, but my children got to go to the schools of their dreams. This was because the private schools have more money to help students afford an education.

Chapter 13: Financial Aid

"YES, VIRGINIA, THERE IS A SANTA CLAUS"

"The beginning of wisdom is: get wisdom."

PROVERBS 4:5

"The important thing to know is what you don't know."

ANON

How Financial Aid Really Works

The biggest mistake most people make, especially those with six-figure incomes, is thinking there is no financial aid available. You think you make too much money or you have too many assets. Let's take the first part of this and explain the difference between need-based aid and merit aid.

Need-based aid is financial aid based upon parent income and assets and student income and assets. Grants are money given that does not have to be paid back. Sounds great, right?

The only problem is that grants are difficult to obtain. All of the money President Obama recently talked about, such as Pell grants, falls under the category of need-based aid. You may be thinking, "Oh, great, Obama has increased the number and size of Pell grants available." Well, to be honest, unless you are earning less than $40,000 a year, you are not going to get any of that money. So for families whose incomes are around $150,000 a year, grants are probably not going to be part of your college funding experience because they are need-based.

The next category of financial aid is loans. There are two different types: government and private. Under government loans there are student direct loans, which, up until recently, were called Stafford loans. There may also be Perkins loans, but the amount and availability varies by state. There is a big misunderstanding regarding these loans. A lot of people say, "I paid my way through school, and therefore my little Suzy and Johnny are going to pay their way." But the only money out there that any student can take out in his or her own name from the government, regardless of EFC, falls under these direct student loans, and it totals just $27,000 over four years. That doesn't even cover one year at the University of Illinois, which is such a popular school in this area. So where are you going to come up with the rest?

The other loans available are parent loans, or PLUS loans, which are parent loans for undergraduate students. For these, only the parents have to sign, but they are expensive. The current interest rate is 8.5 percent, and typically if you earn over $100,000 a year it is not deductible. There is up to a 3-percent origination fee and a 1-percent insurance premium. One good thing former President Bush enacted before he left office was giving parents the ability to defer payments on PLUS loans until the students have stopped going to school full time. However, even though you can defer principal payment, interest is still accruing. So typically when I talk to the parents about PLUS loans I tell them to write PLUS on a piece of paper, put a circle around it, put a line through it, and write 666 all over it, because that is a last resort in my opinion.

Another option is private loans, which are available through private banks as well as the Sally Mae organization. Typically these are loans cosigned by both the student and the parents. The good thing about these loans is their requirement of accountability for the students. Another aspect, which has positive as well as negative implications, is that the interest must be paid during the college years even though you can defer the principal. Since the student is paying the interest while in college, he or she is actually building up a credit history. So when your student graduates from college and needs to buy his or her first car, or rent an apartment, or take out a loan, he or she will have established a credit history.

The other loan, which is actually the cheapest money out there, is the home equity loan. Interest is generally deductible for most families, and it is the least expensive interest. However, with the recent recession, most property values have declined to the point that most families no longer have enough equity available to take out a second mortgage or home equity loan.

I tell all of my families that borrowing money to send their kids to school is fine, but professionally and personally as a planner, I make it a point to ensure parents will be debt-free by the time they retire because there is much less of a strain on retirement resources if they have no debt.

One last point about loans pertaining to students: If your student is going to take out student loans and will co-sign with you, I strongly recommend that the student not take out more loans than their expected first year's salary. For example someone who is going to be a teacher with a salary of $35,000 should not take out any more student loans than $35,000. If your kid has to pay student loans plus a car payment and any other debt, then he or she is going to boomerang on you and have to move back home to survive financially.

The only exception I make is for doctors, lawyers, and dentists. Their earning capacity is so much higher that I don't have a problem if they are going to take out more loans than their first year's salary. The one caution I'd have about the medical profession is for veterinarians, because the usual starting salary is about $65,000.

Merit Aid

Merit aid is financial aid based on academics, athletics, and fine arts rather than income. We encourage parents to look at this because we've had several families over the years who have high incomes and their students have in some cases gotten full-ride scholarships that provide the complete cost of attendance through merit aid.

Some competitive schools, in our area such as the University of Illinois Urbana-Champaign or the University of Michigan, are mostly interested in ACT scores, GPA, and class rank. They are not interested in how many community service hours you have, extracurricular activities, or volunteer hours.

As far as merit aid for athletes, I say this to parents: If you haven't heard from the Division I schools by junior year, you're not going to hear from them. Period. So stop dreaming. However, you still have Division II schools, Division III schools, and the NAIA schools with lots of money to give to students. Technically, however, Division III schools do not give out "athletic" scholarships. But they will give your child money to go there. For example, let's say your child plays football. Most of these private schools have deep pockets, and they will find a way to get your child to go there. They just call it something other than an athletic scholarship.

The key is to start early, and also when getting athletic scholarships, you need to be flexible. The schools will pick you, not the other way around. If your child wants to play, you need to be a little more open about him or her going to a school that is farther away or smaller than you want.

Be careful about selecting a school with the right major. Particular majors can eliminate the opportunity for athletic involvement in college. We had a young lady who was a great soccer player and was recruited, but she wanted to study architecture. Well, there is no way on this planet your student can be both an architecture major and a soccer player! There just isn't time for both.

We had another student who was an incredible golfer and near the top of her class, shooting par in 8th grade, and she also wanted to get into engineering. She was recruited by the University of Michigan. Keep in mind that is a Division I school, and at that level the coaches own you. Well, University of Michigan also has a phenomenal engineering program; it is one of the top ones in the country. That was a disaster. You can't focus on golf, especially with a team that is traveling all over the country, and still maintain your GPA (and sanity); it's not going to happen. Between a rigorous golf schedule and demanding engineering program, she burned out and dropped out after one year.

Most fine arts schools, like schools of design, are not generally well funded and do not have the funds to provide scholarships.

However there are schools around the country that do provide scholarships, such as the Savannah School of Design. If you have a great portfolio and a decent ACT score, they will give you scholarships for both.

Some scholarships are privately funded. These scholarships are often promoted to the public as, "Millions of dollars are available in scholarships that are never used." The reality is that roughly only 1.5 percent of all the money out there comes from private scholarships. So here is typically what is going to happen: All of the schools that your child is accepted to will send you a financial reward letter, and that will tell you exactly how much school is going to cost. When you get those letters I suggest you have two things handy: a letter opener and a paper bag for when you start hyperventilating. As soon as you get off the floor, your first thought is going to be, "OMG, how am I going to pay for this?" and your second thought is going to be to call your high-school counselor or your college admissions counselor and beg for help.

They will tell you to go to www.fastweb.com. Fastweb.com is a clearing house for private scholarships. As a matter of fact if you Google "financial aid," a whole bunch of these are going to pop up. What you'll do is have your child enter his or her characteristics, GPAs, desires, traits, achievements, etc, and then you will get hits back for the private scholarships that fit their profile.

All four of my children are brilliant. (Thank God they have my wife's charm, intelligence, and good looks, because it removes me from considerable responsibility.) My oldest daughter had a 34 on her ACT; a 4.6 GPA on a 4.0 scale; was number three in her class; had all kinds of awards, all kinds of extracurricular activities, and all kinds of leadership; and wanted to go into engineering. (By the way if you have daughters who are good at math, have them look at engineering, because the world is their oyster.) I had Stephanie apply for 25 scholarships through fastweb.com…she got $0.

Now daughter number two, also a great student with a great ACT score, a gifted writer who won a national writing contest, applied to 12 of those scholarships online. She got $0. My sons, Michael and Chris, didn't even bother to apply.

The truth is that a lot of these foundations by law can give the money to their own family for decades before they have to give your child anything. You can thank the IRS for those loopholes. To top it off, much of the money that is available is need- based only. So even if you have a very talented student, if you're a middle class family, it will be very difficult to get some of this private foundation money. And even if you do, the second thing to remember is that most of this money is not renewable. In the past nine years, we've only had two families ever receive money from these scholarships, one for $250, the other for about $1,200. I'm not saying you can't get money there; I am just saying don't spend 99 percent of your time going after 1 percent of the money.

With regard to other scholarships, one of the best places to look is where you work. Many corporations have scholarships for students; also local foundations would have them, as well as places like Sam's Club, Wal-Mart, and Target. The key to this is going to be to keep up with your guidance counselor's office. So whether they put notices on a bulletin board or place them on the Internet, start looking for these scholarships around fall of junior year. Most of them are due sometime around January of senior year.

Keep in mind that these scholarship applications are like sending in a resume for a job application. Be extremely careful in terms of what they are looking for. The foundations will use any excuse whatsoever to not give you the money. For example, if they tell you they want an essay that is 300 words long and you turn in an essay that is 350 words, it will bump you. So whatever specifications they are looking for, whatever topic they are looking for, make sure you stick to the topic, and stick to the word count.

How to Become More Eligible for Financial Aid

Being a business owner provides a lot of loopholes. Number one: paying my kids.

All of my children have worked for me over the years. They can earn up to $5,300 roughly without having to pay income taxes. Paying them lowered my taxes. In addition, I had brochures for my business, and I used my children's pictures in the brochures and paid them royalties on their photos. So that was another way I could take money out of my business and lower my expected family contribution to help them qualify for more need-based aid.

Also by being self-employed, the type of retirement program that I had made a difference. Funding retirement while taking into account the financial aid formula can reap rewards worth thousands. Most people think that the more money you put in your 401Ks, the more you will qualify for need based-aid, which is absolutely false because it is a voluntary contribution. Contributing to your 401Ks, 453Bs, and 457 plans will certainly lower your taxes, but the department of education adds those numbers back into the formula.

Another way to qualify for more financial aid is to reposition your assets so they do not have to be listed on a financial aid form. I discuss this further in the LUC Chapter. In addition, if you have real estate holdings, being able to list them as a business rather than a personal asset will benefit your payments as you will not have to list it on your FAFSA (Free Application for Federal Student Aid) form. An additional way of reducing your (EFC) Expected Family Contribution is by lowering your reportable income through the use of a Deferred Compensation Plan at your workplace. However, be sure to discuss this with your accountant or financial planner first.

The bottom line is there are many ways for business owners, farmers and individuals to reduce the EFC, but I strongly recommend that you sit down with a college planning specialist to see what fits your unique situation and needs.

Chapter 14: Financial Award Letters

"AND THE ENVELOPE, PLEASE"

"He feared that, he would not have
enough for his expenses."

1 MACCABEES 3:30

"Depend on it, Sir, when a man knows
he is to be hanged in a fortnight, it
concentrates his mind wonderfully."

SAMUEL JOHNSON

Every school your student gets accepted to will send you a
financial award letter. The purpose of the letter is to notify you
of the various components of the financial aid package you'll
be receiving, such as scholarships and grants (the free money),
student loans, work study, and parent loans.

Your choices are to accept, deny, or appeal any portion the
offer. Appeal, what's an appeal? Going to college is like buying

a car or house. There's no reason to pay full sticker unless you want to.

That being said, there are several points to be aware of: 1) Some schools out there will not appeal. I consider them part of my terrorist watch list, since negotiation is not part of their vocabulary. 2) You must follow each school's appeal procedures. 3) All schools want to know your final answer by May 1st, so don't procrastinate too long or any extra money will be gone.

When my daughter Stephanie decided she wanted to go into ocean engineering, two schools in Florida appealed to us. Her first and second choices were Florida Atlantic University and Florida Institute of Technology. My brokerage firm's home office was only about two miles away from Florida Atlantic University in Boca Raton and I thought, "Well, that'd be great, I'd be able to see her a fair amount."

Florida Atlantic is large school, with an enrollment of approximately 20,000 students, as opposed to Florida Tech. which only has about 3,000 students. However, every time I walked into Florida Atlantic's financial aid office, even during the summer, there was a line way outside the door. When I finally talked to the financial aid officer, and again I am a professional and I know what I'm doing, I said, "Here's my expected family contribution; can you please give me an example of what your financial aid packages look like? How much we would be able to get in grants?"

"It depends on what your financial budget is," she answered.

"Financial budget?" I asked. "What the heck is a financial budget?"

"Well, sir, it depends on what your budget is."

"Ma'am, I understand grants and loans. I understand Estimated Financial Contribution. I am a Certified College Planning Specialist. Please talk English to me. So here's my EFC; it is $11,000. What is my financial aid package going to look like?"

"It depends on what your budget is."

It felt like I was talking to a wall. There was no flexibility and I could not get around what was going on, and at the time Florida Atlantic was Stephanie's number one choice. We had met with the admissions counselor and she had told Stephanie that because of her ACT and GPA, she would get free tuition.

Then I got the financial award letter from Florida Atlantic and the bill was a heck of a lot higher than I thought it was supposed to be. There was definitely something wrong with this. Well, what happened was there was a whole extra surcharge since she was going to be taking 18 credit hours; we had to pay out-of-state tuition for six of the hours. So I called the admissions office and said that there must be some kind of mistake because we had received the financial award letter and were being billed for six credit hours.

I said, "You told us that it would be free tuition." She said, "Oh, absolutely, Mr. Groleau. You are going to be getting free tuition." I said, "Well, that's not what it says in the letter." So we got on the phone with the head of the engineering department and told him that when we visited, we were told Stephanie would be receiving free tuition.

"Oh yes, Mr. Groleau. You are receiving free tuition."

"No, I'm not."

"Yes, you are."

"No, I'm not."

"Yes, you are."

So I faxed both of them the financial award letter and they were both kind of stunned and said they would get back to us. Well, they didn't, so I called and asked what was going on because we needed to make a decision. Then I had a four-way conference call with the admissions office, the head of the engineering department, and the financial aid officer. Here is where the rubber met the road. The financial aid officer said, "No, she gets free tuition for 12 hours a semester and you'll have to pay out-of-state rates for anything over 12 hours a semester".

Well, needless to say, I was not happy. So we tried to negotiate this change and they would say, "We will get back to you, Mr. Groleau. We are sorry for the miscommunication. We will work this out."

I waited and waited and finally, I said, "Stephanie, you'd better call those other schools." Thankfully, she called Florida Institute of Technology and they honored the award they had promised her and that's where she went. In addition, when I not-so-casually mentioned that I was going to have three kids in college at the same time with Shireen starting next year, FIT kicked in another $1,500 per year. So, I just want you to be aware that if your gut is telling you there is an issue with the school, then you know what, follow your gut. The important point is that it took more than one visit to figure this out.

Here are some key points to remember as you consider using the appeals process for your own student.

A. **Reasons to appeal fall under 3 categories:**

    1) Financial loss due to unemployment, divorce, bankruptcy, stock market losses, etc.

    2) High medical expenses for someone in the family.

    3) Competitive offers from other schools.

B. **How to appeal:**

    1) Ask what the school's appeals process is.

    2) Write down your problem.

    3) State what your "magic" number is.

    4) What do you want the school to do.

I always prefer face-to-face if possible because it's harder to say "no" in person. If you send a letter, use second day delivery. Expect a reply in 10 days; if you don't get one, CALL!!

C. **Reasons why appeals fail:**

    1) Student not competitive.

    2) Letter too long.

3) Too many talking points.

4) Lack of persistence.

5) College doesn't care.

6) Not enough specifics.

7) No documentation.

8) Misrepresentation of facts.

9) Not read by the right person.

10) Poorly written.

Chapter 15: Making the Final College Choice

THRIVING VS. SURVIVING

"But if any of you lacks wisdom, he should ask God."

JAMES 1:5

"Nothing can bring you to happiness but yourself."

RALPH WALDO EMERSON

Each Child Is as Unique as a Snowflake

BY LAYLA

Any parent with more than one child can attest to the above statement. We are often surprised by how our own four children, raised by the same two parents in the same home, can be so different. Each has his or her own talents, temperament, passions, and personality. So when it comes to college choices, unfortunately, one size does not fit all.

The cold, long Chicago winters really bothered Stephanie, and her free spirit yearned for the beach. Besides, a major in ocean engineering requires some proximity to a body of water! A small tech school on the ocean in Florida was her final choice. However, her sister Shireen is our city girl. She is a highly social person and is drawn to the excitement of city life. She chose a mid-sized Catholic school in the city with a reputation for its strong business program.

Michael and Christopher, on the other hand, both choose the same school, a mid-sized Catholic college with a fantastic engineering department and a reputation for the most active campus ministry in the country! They had thrived in their high school youth group, and they really wanted a place that could feed their faith, a place where they could meet like-minded friends. While John and I had often dreamed of all our children going to the same college, perhaps our alma mater, it turned out that that scenario wouldn't have been well suited for each of the unique talents and personalities of our children.

Focus on the Right College or Thriving vs. Surviving

Once your child's career choice is solidified, then you can focus on finding the right college. The "right" college means a lot of things, but ultimately it's finding the school where your child is going to thrive. In my own college career—or I should say "almost" college careers—I started off at a big school, the University of Maine at Orono, with an undergrad population of 10,000 students. Put that against my high school graduating class of 64 at St. Dominic's High School in Lewiston, Maine. What a culture shock that was. Going from 400 students in the school to 10,000 was a huge change. Why did I pick UMO? I dunno; a few of my friends were going there and it was far from home.

Looking back after going through Career Vision, I realize that my personality is much more suited to a small school with hands-on learning versus academic, and with interactive classrooms versus lecture halls. When I later transferred to the University of Maine in Farmington, with its campus of 1,500 students, my GPA went from a 2.5 to a 3.9 in one semester. I attribute part of that to the campus atmosphere and part to a couple of professors who truly inspired me to do my best. One in particular, Dr. Robert Martin, is to this day one of the best professors I ever had. He just had an ability to pull the best out of me. I made high honors every year after that all the way through grad school. So finding the right professors is important for a good fit.

Keep this in mind when picking a college. Take the time to figure out your child's learning style. Is she OK with lecture halls or does she need smaller class sizes? Is she OK with academic learning, or does she need more hands-on learning?

Then there is the matter of grad assistants and TAs versus actual professors. These are not insignificant points; they can make huge differences in your child's academic career and can make the difference between thriving and surviving. Students should fall in love with a school, thriving environmentally, academically, and especially for parents, financially. It takes time to determine what will be the best environment for your child to thrive in.

Parents, I want to put this in perspective. How many of you know people (you may even be one of them) who can't stand what they're doing at work? How many of you know people who just clock in and out every day? How many people do you know who truly love what they're doing in their careers? Based on the informal polling of my clients I've conducted through the years, not many. Is that what you want for your kids? Do you want to spend all that money sending them to some school that was selected based on where their best friends are going or on the fact that they have a good football team? Don't you want them truly loving their lives and being contributors to their own personal growth? Then please spend the time to find out which college will have the environment to foster their thriving.

For your student, let me present this to him or her from a different perspective. Think about your favorite class or teacher(s) in school. Now contrast that with your least favorite classes or teachers. Which one of these sets of teachers would you prefer to spend four years of college with?

Every year we will have students go through the Career Vision process who are advised to go to a small school. They disagree, saying they want to go to a Big Ten school. By the end of the semester, too many of them are back home, realizing their school choice was a disaster. It is really crucial that you know your child's learning style to find where he or she is going to thrive.

If you know your child doesn't have street smarts, then don't pick an inner city school unless your child plans to take a protection class. Shireen's school was located in a rather nasty section of Chicago, and she was assaulted three times during her four years. Thankfully she wasn't hurt, just scared. Some of the schools in inner cities are not in very nice areas, and you and your student need to be aware of that and take appropriate measures such as a self-defense class or making sure to carry things like pepper spray. Whatever it is, keep in mind that if you go to an inner city school you are going to be in a city environment, and you need to have some common sense and street smarts.

When selecting colleges, one thing for your child to keep in mind is whether he or she will prefer an urban or rural environment. Michael and Christopher didn't really care, Stephanie wanted to be near the beach, and Shireen had to be in Chicago. Some students are okay with a big school, while others need a small school. That's what you want to look for in a college.

On surveys about what had the most influence on their college careers, most graduating seniors do not say it was football games or basketball games or cheerleaders or parties. 99 percent of the time it was one or two professors who changed their lives. Look for a school where the professors are going to be mentors for your kids.

You also want to look in terms of your child's learning style. Is he going to be OK in an auditorium with 500 kids? Or will he be better with small classroom sizes? Is he OK with lecture-style learning, or does he need more interactive classrooms? For me, I needed small classrooms, hands-on learning, and interactive classroom styles. That's when I really grew, blossomed, and thrived as a student.

Chapter 16: How to Pay for College

L.U.C. (LIQUIDITY, USE AND CONTROL)

"For all their riches, if mortals do not have wisdom, they perish like the beasts."

PSALM 49:4

"A wise man will make more opportunities than he finds."

SIR FRANCIS BACON

In this section I want to discuss savings vehicles: how to pay for college by saving and investing your money wisely, avoiding common pitfalls. I'm not going to make this book into an exhaustive resource on how to save or invest for college. You can go online and find plenty of material on that subject. Instead I will highlight the most common funding vehicles used by most families.

There are three points that should be used as a benchmark no matter what vehicle you intend to use. They are Liquidity,

Use, and Control. For example, you could take a loan from your 401k to pay for college. However, you are limited to 50% or 50k, whichever is less (limited liquidity), but you can use it for anything. In terms of control, though, you must start paying it back immediately within five years. That could seriously affect your remaining cash flow to pay for school.

The first option is what is known as the Coverdell ESA (formerly known as the Education IRA). Let's talk about some of its pluses and minuses.

The Coverdell ESA was established in 2002. Under the current design, you can use it to pay for any of your child's educational and related expenses, so these monies are not limited just to college expenses. However, that rule is expected to change. Withdrawals can still be used for elementary and secondary education for the time being. The limitations are that you can only put in $2,000 per year per child, from all sources. So, if Grandma and Grandpa put in $2,000 a year, you cannot add to that. The funds do grow tax-deferred and can be withdrawn tax-free for educational expenses. They can be invested stocks, bonds, mutual funds, CDs, etc. So plusses are tax-free growth, and minuses are limited contributions of $2,000 per year.

The next savings vehicle is an IRA, which you can fund in one of two ways. You can use your own IRA to pay for college, or you can establish IRAs in your children's names if they have income to allow it. If you use the funds to pay for college expenses, the good news is that you do not have to pay the additional 10 percent penalty if you are under 59 ½. The bad news is that the growth, or capital gains, comes out first and is taxed as ordinary income. So until you take enough out to reduce your cost bases, you will be paying taxes on that money. The danger of taking an IRA withdrawal is that since it counts as ordinary income, the increased income will *decrease* your eligibility for need-based financial aid. One family I met with recently was going to take an IRA withdrawal to help pay for college. The family's income was approximately $70,000 with an Expected Family Contribution of $8,300. Taking $30,000 out of their IRA would have increased their EFC to over $30,000. They would have lost $22,000 per year in financial aid. They'd be far better off borrowing the money while their child is in school and then withdrawing from the IRA later to pay off the loans.

A Roth IRA, on the other hand, can also be used for college, and unlike a regular IRA, your contributions come out first. So if you put $10,000 into a Roth IRA and it's now worth $20,000, your original $10,000 comes out tax-free, provided it has met the five-year requirement. If you're going to use this as a college-fund vehicle, you need to start the process early enough because it must be open for a minimum of five years before any withdrawals. In other words, if you opened a Roth in 2007 and you didn't contribute any money in it until 2011, you could still withdraw your contributions in 2012, tax-free.

Any withdrawals above your original cost basis will be taxed as ordinary income but does avoid the 10-percent penalty.

Let's turn to 529 savings plans. These college funding vehicles certainly caught the world by storm...for a while. They were considered to be the greatest idea since sliced bread, but in my opinion, the bloom has fallen from the rose. The good news is that in a 529 plan, the money you put in you can pull out tax-free, and you can withdraw any deposits tax-free. Additionally, gains in the account are tax-exempt provided withdrawals are used for qualified college expenses. You have to be careful about what "qualified" means. If your child needs a laptop, for example, that does not necessarily count as a qualified expense. If your child needs a car to get to school, that definitely does not count as qualified. Then what does count as qualified??

Qualified higher education expenses (QHEE) includes tuition, fees, books, supplies, equipment required for study at any accredited college, and the additional expenses of a "special needs" beneficiary. For students who are pursuing a degree on at least a half-time basis, QHEE also includes a limited amount of room and board. Off-campus housing costs are covered up to the allowance for room and board that the college includes in its cost of attendance for federal financial-aid purposes. The cost of computer technology, related equipment, and/or related services such as internet access is also included. The technology, equipment, or services qualify if they are used by the beneficiary of the plan and the beneficiary's family during any of the years the beneficiary is enrolled at an eligible educational institution. However, you must subtract any grants, scholarships, or discounts.

You *cannot* include the following expenses:

- ✔ Insurance, sports or club activity fees, and many other types of fees that may be charged to your students but are not required as a condition of enrollment.

- ✔ A computer, unless the institution requires that students have their own computers.

- ✔ Transportation costs.

- ✔ Repayment of student loans or interest.

- ✔ Room and board costs in excess of the amount the school includes in its "cost of attendance" figures for federal financial aid purposes. If your student is living off campus, ask the financial aid department for the room and board allowance for students living at home with parents, or living elsewhere off campus, as the case may be. If the student is living in campus-owned dormitories, the amount you can include in QHEE is the amount the school charges for its room and board.

The advantages are that you can put in up to $13,000 annually, or a lump sum of $65,000, but then you cannot contribute for the next four years to avoid paying a gift tax. Amounts are doubled if filing a joint tax return. Another feature in 529 plans allows you to change beneficiaries. For example, let's say you have three children, and you did so well with scholarships for Suzy, your oldest child, that you did not use all of her 529 plan money. There are no tax consequences for changing the beneficiary to another family member, so you can use the money for another child's education. If you have no more children you can assign as beneficiary, you can use this for other family members. The disadvantages of the 529 plan are that, in terms of the title of the chapter (Liquidity, Use, and Control), you can really only use this for college. If you use this for something other than qualified college expenses, the funds you take out are taxable, and a 10% penalty is applied to it.

Control is another key area, because a majority of the 529 plans have limited investment options. Even the most option has no guarantees. For example here in Illinois, we have something called the Bright Start program. If you felt the world's economy was going to hell in a handbasket, and you picked the most conservative investment, which is called the protected principal plan, you'd think that your money was going to be safe. When you explore further, it turns out the protected principal option under "normal circumstances" would protect your principal against loss. But given the circumstances of the past few years, it would be a mistake to assume your principal would be absolutely guaranteed.

Another negative about the 529 investment plans is that you can only make one investment change per year. So if you predicted back in August 2008 that the market was starting to go in the toilet, and you put your assets in the most conservative position, then several months later in March 2009 when the market hit rock bottom, you could not take advantage of buying opportunities until August 2009. So in a volatile market, which we may be experiencing for the next few years based upon past history for the length of bear markets, there is little control over a vehicle like that.

Another version of the 529 is the prepaid tuition plan. These work by signing up on a contractual basis either lump sum, or annual or monthly payments. You're purchasing future tuition (and fees) at today's prices. The state you purchase these in "guarantees" that they will provide the number of semesters you've purchased for your child in the year he or she graduates. In theory, it's a great idea, especially since the rising cost of a college education has surpassed even that of health care! If you were to assume a 6 percent increase of college expenses, where else can you get 6 percent return on your money? Nowhere, really.

But I have concerns about this type of vehicle. First, an independent audit of all the prepaid tuition plans published a couple of years ago stated that only 17 states were fully capable of meeting the funding obligations of the students. My own state of Illinois was not one of them (no big surprise there considering Illinois has consistently ranked 48th or worse in the United States for funding higher education). When I called the department responsible for the prepaid tuition program, they vehemently denied that there would be any forfeiture on their part. When I quoted the article, they just kept saying that the state of Illinois would stand behind its obligation. Illinois and other states finally admitted publically this year that they have concerns about making full payment.

Just recently an article in The Chicago Tribune came down hard on the College Illinois! Plan. It brought out the fact that the state of Illinois does not actually guarantee the contracts to cover the full cost. The article also emphasized that the investment fund backing the plan has fallen far short and that new "investors" will have to pay a higher amount to cover the costs of those who started years ago. Sounds a bit like Social Security, doesn't it?

Another concern I have is the cost differentials in tuition among the various campuses. In Illinois, for example, the cost of tuition at the flagship campus in Urbana-Champaign is approximately $19,000/year. At the Eastern Illinois campus, tuition is only $8,000/yr. Well, if you purchased eight semesters of Urbana-Champaign prepaid and your child attends the Eastern Illinois campus, you do not get a refund because you didn't go to University of Illinois Urbana-Champaign. Also, if you decide to attend a private school or an out-of-state college, you will receive the average of all the Illinois state university tuitions applied to wherever you attend. Recently, the College Illinois! Plan has instated changes enabling you to purchase semesters just for/or excluding the Urbana campus. My concern is that this puts a lot of pressure on students to attend a school which may not be a great fit for them.

Next on the list are the UTMAs and UGMAs. UTMA stands for Unified Trust for Minors Act, which is in Illinois and several other states, and UGMA stands for Unified Gift for Minors Act, which is used in the remaining states. The difference is that in the UGMA, the assets are available to the child at age 18, and with the UTMA, the assets are available to the child at age 21. In terms of liquidity, you can pretty much invest in whatever you like with these. But you as the parent or guardian do have fiduciary responsibility. What does this mean? I remember a family who invested their child's UTMA account in gold stocks, right when gold was about $800 an ounce in the 1980s, and it only went in one direction from there—-down. So the child's fund, which had been at about $25,000, eventually went down to about $6,200, which is not anywhere near what anybody thought, and the child actually sued the parent and won. Even though you have unlimited access to investments, you need to exercise care in regard to how those assets are invested. Now the problem with using UTMAs or UGMAs is that at age 18 or 21 (depending on which type you have) if your child knows about that fund and has reached the age of majority, or control, and decides he or she wants to go buy a Mustang convertible with it or a 72-inch big screen TV or whatever, there are no restrictions.

With regard to annuities, there are several kinds, and these are issued from a life insurance company. There are equity-indexed annuities, fixed annuities, and variable annuities. The liquidity part is an issue because many annuities have long surrender charges. Typically fixed annuities and equity-indexed annuities will have surrender charges lasting at least eight years, which makes them impractical for most people to use for college. They are tax-deferred, but again liquidity is a problem. Since they are tax-deferred, they are taxed as ordinary income along with a ten-percent penalty until the owner of the annuity is over 59 ½.

As far as permanent life insurance, there are several different types: whole life, universal life, equity-indexed universal life, and variable life. If we apply the L.U.C. formula, liquidity is a problem because most permanent life insurance policies do not break even until you have them for 15 years. In other words, the equity in the policy does not equal the total premiums paid until 15 years have elapsed. This makes it impractical for college unless you start this process very early.

However, there are some companies which offer the option of "supercharging" your life insurance by adding extra money. For example, some of the whole life companies will allow you to buy what are called "paid up additions" and cause the break to occur much earlier. More specifically, when you buy a typical life insurance contract you are purchasing the largest death benefit for the least amount of premium. When you do that it takes 15 years to break even because you are focused on death benefit. You are getting a return, but you are focusing on death benefit. In addition, the expenses are very high. The insurance agents are typically paid a dollar or more in commission for every dollar of premium in the first year. So it takes a while to make up the cost of commission, underwriting, and other expenses. If you supercharge the contract and shove as much money in there as possible, the goal is to get the lowest death benefit in order to get the highest return possible.

By using paid-up additions, the majority of your money is being focused on the return side rather than the death-benefit side, and for the majority of your money you are only paying two-and-a-half cents commission for every dollar of premium, rather than a dollar or more of commission for every dollar of premium. So this can cause your break-even point to occur anywhere between your first and fifth years. I used this vehicle in my own family and for several of my clients, and it can be constructed in various ways to fit individual needs.

All of these vehicles I've talked about — the Coverdells, IRAs, Roth IRAs, 529s, annuities and life insurance — generally can be compared in a grid which is available on our website.

The key question is if you are going to create your own personal family bank, what are the characteristics you want for your money? Now of course, it is not going to be chartered like Bank of America, or Fifth Third Bank, but your wealthy families create these- "banks." They're called trusts. Whatever type of bank it is, whether a real one like the Carnegies have or a trust that you've set up, the goal is that you want to plan out the characteristics of your "bank", so that if you want to use the money for college, and perhaps use whatever's left after college for retirement or to purchase cars, you get to decide what you want to use the money in the bank for.

There are two ways to fill up this bank. One is by adding a lump sum, and the other is by adding to it monthly or annually. So the characteristics to grade all these different vehicles are as follows:

1. Competitive rate of return.

2. Liquidity. Be aware of 12b1 fees, surrender charges, penalties, or market volatility (such as real estate).

3. Safety. If you're going to need the money in the next five years, for example, you should not be putting this money at risk. Guaranteed principle might be a plus.

4. Taxable versus tax-deferred or tax-free.

5.   FAFSA invisible. Depending upon your eligibility for need-based aid, you might consider using a vehicle that will protect your assets from the prying eyes of the financial aid forms.

As you look at the above characteristics of your "bank" you might be saying to yourself, "I want something that will provide all five." In that case, there are only two vehicles that accomplish all of the above. They are either annuities or life insurance. I strongly recommend that before you start any college funding vehicle or "bank", sit down with a certified college planning specialist who is also a financial planner so you can thoroughly examine all the options from both the financial aid as well as financial planning side of the equation.

Chapter 17: High School Internships, Job-Shadowing, and Informational Interviews

"I ALWAYS WANTED TO BE ... A LUMBERJACK!"

"So that one who belongs to God may be competent, equipped for every good work."

2 TIMOTHY 3:17

"I like work, it fascinates me, I can sit and look at it for hours."

JEROME K. JEROME

Talking about your values, interests, and abilities certainly can help create a menu of career opportunities geared toward your unique personality. To take it a step further, take the time to investigate the most promising of these options.

The easiest way to get a clearer picture of what each career is really like is to interview people actually working in these areas. This is not a formal interview, but a casual conversation to answer any questions you might have. You might want to start with friends and relatives for contacts in various careers.

High school counselors and professional career counselors can also be very helpful with providing contacts. First, call and introduce yourself, explaining your interest in the profession. Then ask if it would be convenient to speak to your contact for ten to fifteen minutes. This can be done at the place of business, over lunch at a local restaurant, or even on the telephone. Most professionals are more than happy to talk about their work. These are truly the best people to offer insight.

If after an initial interview you want to investigate more, let job-shadowing show you what a day in the life at this job will feel like. Take advantage of any "Take Your Kid to Work Day" your school or parents' place of employment offers. You can even go with someone else's parent or a neighbor if you find a career that might be of some interest to you. Job-shadowing could be for just one day, or even a week, depending on the time you have available and the opportunities offered by the professional you are shadowing.

The closest thing to actually working in a given profession is taking on an internship. Some internships are available to high school students, such as spending a few hours in a classroom with a teacher. Some high schools offer job co-ops, but mostly in fields that do not require a college degree, like food service, retail, or mechanical work. Typically in high school, after-school or summer jobs in a related field to your interest might be your best option. Most internships are offered to college students during the school year or the summer. These are set up through the college with local business partners. If you are interested in an internship that your college has not offered, you can certainly ask your college professors or advisor for help in setting up one that is more specifically meets your needs. In an internship, your co-workers will truly "show you the ropes." You will experience, first-hand, the joys and challenges of that particular career. Keep in mind, of course, that this is only one experience, and not necessarily representative of every working atmosphere in this field.

My daughter Shireen, who graduated with a marketing degree, had five job offers, and all but one came from internships she had. Internships are vital to making your child as marketable as possible.

This is a long preamble to say that while you are interviewing the colleges, every single college is going to tell you "of course we have internships!" The follow-up question is, "Mr. President, what support do you give to help students find internships?" You want to keep drilling down with those types of questions to make sure you are going to get the support you need. The school my daughter attended pretty much just put the internships up on a bulletin board. Learning to interview schools and having the right questions is absolutely vital.

Since internships in college are absolutely crucial, one of the things you want to find out is whether you are in an area where internships are available. One of my favorite schools in Illinois, for example, is Knox College, an awesome school. It's known as a "pre" school — pre-med, pre-law, pre-vet, pre-dental — but it's in Galesburg, IL, which is in the middle of a cornfield. If you want to get an internship working for a corporation, you might have some struggles because of their location. It does not necessarily mean that this college doesn't have good internships, but inquire about their networking capabilities to help you get good internships.

Chapter 18: Parent and Student Case Studies

"THE GOOD, THE BAD..."

"For he who despises wisdom and
instruction is doomed."

WISDOM 3:11

"Nothing that is worth knowing can be taught."

OSCAR WILDE

So, what does it take to be successful? How can a student set
him or herself apart from the pack? Is a great education enough?
Following are a group of case students showing the good and
bad planning scenarios.

The Good

STUDENT CASE STUDY #1
A Tale of Two Siblings

In this particular family the parents had a son and daughter one year apart in high school. Both students went through Career Vision to find out what field they should be looking at, and healthcare came up as the number one choice for both. The son could not decide between becoming a physician or veterinarian. He decided to work in a vet clinic to get experience and earn money. At my recommendation he and his sister signed up to take a certified nurse assistant class which would give them the ability to work in a hospital, clinic, or doctor's office while in college.

In researching the schools both Tom and Sue liked the pre-med program at St. Louis University. One of the appealing factors was that St. Louis University would get them on the hospital floor in their freshman year to get as much experience as possible.

During that year Tom discovered as result of his hospital floor time that he really wanted to work with animals instead. The vet clinic owner who had been impressed with Tom's work ethic and pet "bedside manner" offered him a partnership for when he graduates from vet school. Because of the accelerated pre-vet program at St. Louis he was able to finish in three years instead of four and start vet school one year earlier, which will be a huge savings for the family.

Once Sue, the daughter, had finished her certified nursing assistant class, she was hired to work at a doctors' clinic. The head physician was so impressed with her focus and purpose that he even offered to sponsor her through medical school.

PARENT CASE STUDY #1
The Hoarders

Just as some people hoard junk, we had a family that hoarded financial instruments. They had over a dozen and a half CD's scattered in six banks in three different states, five different brokerage accounts, four IRA's for each spouse and two Roth IRA's for each. It looked like something out of a hoarders' reality TV show. Don't get me wrong. Both parents were very bright—one a psychologist, the other a nurse. They were great savers, just not great organizers.

Their expected family contribution (EFC) was $37,000 for their two sons for college. First, we repositioned their assets in order to lower their EFC to $17,000. This automatically qualified them for more financial aid. Then we worked on their cash flow and their retirement. The final result was that they would be able to afford $18,000 per year, out-of-pocket, for each student, qualify for need-based aid, and still get to retire at their desired retirement age of 66 for the husband and 65 for the wife. An interesting note here is that we were also able to build in a financial cushion for their son who has spina bifida. This cushion is there for any special needs that might arise. Their son is a very active young man who plays both competitive basketball in a wheel chair and also ice hockey on a sled, so you can imagine there are some bigger expenses we were able to help them plan for while still accomplishing their retirement goals.

PARENT CASE STUDY #2
Just Do It ... Right the First Time

As opposed to the previous family who required some major re-organizing and planning, this family just did everything right from the beginning. They came up with their goals. They developed a solid plan, and they implemented that plan well.

They had two sons, Mark and Jim, who were two years apart. Both parents had great jobs, one in engineering, one in marketing. Both children went through Career Vision. Mark, the older son, through researching his job options and job-shadowing, narrowed his major down to chemical engineering. There was great communication between Mark and our counselors to make sure that all the timelines were met.

Mark and his parents visited schools of varying size and academic environment to get a good picture of their options. They wanted to ensure a well thought-out decision. They decided on The University of Minnesota because of their great reputation for chemical engineering and the opportunities for internships in the Twin Cities area. Because Mark is an outstanding student with a great GPA and test scores, The University of Minnesota offered him in-state tuition. Because of the parents' cash flow planning, the in-state cost of attendance at The University of Minnesota was well within their range of affordability.

The Bad

STUDENT CASE STUDY #1
It's Not Just the Degree

Amanda went to a top Midwestern school, Illinois Wesleyan. Amanda chose Illinois Wesleyan because of the reputation for high academic standards and job placement. Knowing that she loved writing and history, she did a double-major. Her dream was to use her people skills and work in a corporation in public relations or to become a journalist. Upon graduating with a 3.5 GPA, Amanda moved to Las Vegas to be near her fiancé. Since graduation and moving a year ago, she has struggled to find a job. Amanda has used on-line job search tools such as Career Builder and has been looking on company websites. How does a student who studied hard, received great grades, and volunteered end up with an education and no job?

One big lesson Amanda would pass along: "I wish I would have looked at the internship rates at the college and in the majors that I chose. I did not know how imperative an internship would be. Now, as I struggle to look for a job, I realize that an internship would have provided me the experience I need to land a job."

Amanda has the same struggle that many college graduates face, a great education, but no experience. In a tight economy, employers are looking for, and can easily find, candidates who have experience. The answer is to research and participate in as many internships as possible. Not only do internships provide experience, but you will also meet individuals in your field who can help you land that important first job.

"I graduated with a double major with a good GPA, and I cannot find a professional-level job. Every place I apply says that I do not have enough experience to work for them, even though I am not sure how I am ever supposed to get experience if I am not able to start anywhere. After graduating from college, I worked at two different minimum-wage jobs I could have done in high school just to make some sort of money to pay off my student loans. All of my friends are in the same position, as well. I am currently thinking of going back to graduate school to get a higher degree. I am worried, though, that I will add on a lot more student loans, and still be unable to get a good job after I graduate from there."

STUDENT CASE STUDY #2
I Can Do It Myself

Adam was an extremely bright student who graduated second in his class, with Dad an engineer and Mom a physician. Adam also went through Career Vision, where he was strongly advised not to attend a large school, but rather a small one where he would thrive. However Adam decided that no matter what, he was going to go to a Big Ten school to study engineering.

Because of HIPPA laws Adam's parents were not made aware of their son's struggles and did not find out that he had flunked out of the engineering program until two weeks before the next year's tuition was due. You can imagine the conversations at the dinner table that night.

Adam was so shell-shocked by his experience that he just could not pull himself out of an emotional rut. He attended community college for the next year while researching schools that would be a better fit. He settled on Valparaiso with a student body of approximately 4,000 instead of the 40,000 from his first school.

The good news is that he is now making Dean's List and is thriving. The bad news is that because of his disastrous first year the scholarship he received at Valpraiso is dramatically less than it would have been if he had gone there in the first place.

PARENT CASE STUDY #1
Can You Hear Me Now?

These parents were divorced with the children living with the mother. The husband had a great job. The relationship between the parents was acrimonious at best. Even though they had been divorced for years, the ex-wife not only blamed her ex for the past but for her current woes. Because the children were living with the mother, the financial aid form only required the mother's information. Since she was going to school full-time and only minimally employed, she had the potential for an expected family contribution (EFC) of $1,600 provided we repositioned the $400,000 in assets she received from the divorce settlement.

As a result of the $400,000 in assets, her current EFC was $36,400. However every attempt to get the ex-wife into my office or on the phone was always met with comments like, "I'm too busy. I don't have time."

When I finally was able to present my strategy to reduce her EFC, she took the material home, gave it a cursory glance, and said, "I don't understand what you are suggesting and I don't have time." Her ex-husband was not able to convince her for all of us to sit down in the same room and calmly discuss a plan to minimize assets to pay for college. They have approximately $80,000 in additional monies set aside for each of their two children. The son, Fred Junior, decided to attend George Washington University, with a $61,000 cost of attendance yearly. Although Fred Jr. did get scholarships, the parents still had to come up with $40,000 out of pocket each year to come up with the difference. The bottom line is that if the mother had co-operated, the funds they had set aside would have covered all four years of undergraduate school and a year of graduate school. Instead the college funds were used up in two years and, of course, any assets the mother had were in great jeopardy.

PARENT CASE STUDY #2
The Perfect Storm

My office is often used as a quasi-confessional. I often tell people that there is nothing they can tell me that I have not heard before. But every once in a while I have to eat my words. In this instance I had a father whom I will call Dick, who was a building contractor going through a rough time because of the economy. But when times were good he had been able to put money away into his retirement plans. Because of the slowdown in the economy Dick had started day-trading to try to increase his revenue, but had been keeping his side of the finances a secret from his wife Irene.

When she approached Dick and questioned how he was going to pay for college for their daughter and son, he told her he had a trust fund and not to worry about it. He would not give her any specifics. Dick was often unwilling to come to my office to meet with me and his wife. When I threatened to sever my relationship with the family, he finally came into my office. The ensuing discussion was both illuminating and disturbing.

It turned out that the so-called "trust fund" was actually his retirement plan with a current balance of $350,000. That's the good news. The bad news is that he has not contributed to his plan for the last four years because of the economy. Normally, that amount of money would put them on track to achieve their retirement goals, except that he has not contributed to his plan for the past four years. Now enter the daughter, Cathy, where things get really bizarre.

Cathy had her heart set on attending Purdue University for a cost of $37,000 per year in order to get her teaching certificate. She could have gotten a degree and a teaching certificate in Illinois for $22,000 a year. However, what she really wanted was to have her own breeding barn to raise horses. When I asked the parents why she wasn't applying to The University of Findlay or William Woods, which specialize in equestrian studies and would have thrown money at her, the parents responded that those two schools were too small. I asked them when Cathy had visited the schools to make that determination, and they replied that she had not visited either.

Here comes the Titanic crash. Irene then told me that Dick had promised Cathy that she could go to Purdue. He was willing to use up almost half of his retirement plan to pay for his daughter's college education, in spite of my warnings that he would never be able to make that up again. Basically, in this case Mom and Dad are willing to let their children dictate their future financial well-being. I hope Cathy remembers this moment when Mom and Dad have to move in with her when they retire! After I forced the husband to "fess up" to the family's true financial picture, he now refuses to come back to the office to figure out how he and his wife are actually going to pay for school without dramatically limiting their financial future.

Chapter 19: Cash Flow, Debt, etc.

"... AND THE UGLY"

"Go not surely beyond your means; think
any pledge a debt you must pay."

SIRACH 8:13

"Annual income 20 pounds, annual expenditure
nineteen nineteen six, result happiness. Annual
income 20 pounds, annual expenditure twenty
pound ought and six, result misery."

CHARLES DICKENS

In the course of writing this book I have used material from both my family and my planning practice. However, in this case, I wanted to share with you a story so compelling that I thought it should be told directly from the source—one of my clients. I hope it will help you make wiser decisions with regard to acquiring and managing credit.

For confidentiality purposes I will just refer to this chapter's author as MR.K, a bank officer and portfolio manager with an MBA. While MR.K's story is sad and disturbing it is certainly not unique. In the twenty-five years I have been a planner, not a week goes by without someone coming into my office under similar circumstances. When these clients disclose to me their similar credit situations they often feel ashamed. I hope this story will provide you with the courage if you are in a similar situation to speak up and reach out knowing you are not alone.

MR.K's Story:

The first segment I am going to talk about is credit. What is it, why is it important, how does it work, what needs does it fill, and then I am going to talk about problems people get into when using credit and abusing credit, not understanding it. Before going further I am going to give a little personal example that people might be able to relate to, and then I am going to talk about credit.

A PERSONAL STORY:
Good Intentions, Bad Consequences...

When I was in high school, I began to take an interest in finance and having access to credit. I thought that someday having a large credit line would be an indication of who I was. Then, while I was studying finance in college, I studied banking, and I thought that I understood credit. What I understood was that I needed to establish credit, and the more credit I had available to me the better risk I would be considered, and the more access to capital I would have for investments for business opportunities in the future. So I opened my first credit card and probably was extended $500 of credit. I made purchases and would pay off my balances on time.

After I had my first card, I applied for other cards. Once you have one credit card you'll find that Visa, MasterCard, and all the different banks will market, advertise and offer you even more credit cards; so I started receiving new credit cards from different companies. I accepted them because I thought that was going to be good… I had more credit available to me. Then I started getting direct mail pieces encouraging me to transfer balances from one credit card company to a different credit card company, and they would often offer rates that were 0 percent or very low to influence me to switch over and transfer my balances. For a long period of time I was able to make my payments on time and not abuse credit; however, there came a point, and this happens to many people, when there were red flags that had I noted, I could have prevented quite a few problems.

The Beginning with Credit

I started to make purchases and then rather than pay the entire balance off immediately, I would tell myself, "I'll pay it off over two or three months." Well, every month I didn't pay it off, my balance accrued interest. And the interest rate that I had to pay on a credit card was often 15 or 18 percent or more. So each month that I didn't pay off the balance in full, not only did I have the balance remaining to pay off, but I also had 15 percent or higher in interest rate charges that I had to pay. In the early days I would pay off over three or four months and everything would be fine. But I continued to develop bad habits, which caused further problems.

At one point, I had credit available to me of $40,000 or $50,000. I would try not to use all of the credit and maintain that as capital available to me for the future. But in my case, there was a stock market sell-off that took place somewhere between 1996 and 1998, and I felt that I could make money and convinced myself that it would be OK to take cash advances from credit cards and put that money into the market. I took about $5,000 or $7,000 of money and put that into the market. At first I was making money off short-term trades, but eventually they started to lose money, and I kept the balances on my credit cards while I was trying to make money in the market.

What this caused to happen was that my balances would roll over every month, and then rather than having an amount due of what I borrowed, I would have to pay back not only what I borrowed, but then an additional 18 percent interest. That interest rate accumulated so that every month I kept my balances unpaid in full, I had to pay more back to the credit card company than I had borrowed.

My problems stemmed from not understanding what credit was and not knowing how to use credit properly. I can also claim my marriage had some responsibility. During the course of our marriage (we've been married over 21 years) we've had totally different views on what money is, how to use it, and what credit is and how to use it. All I can suggest to you is that the conversation needs to be as open and on the table in a marriage as the discussion about what to do on a Friday night or what to eat for dinner. It's an uncomfortable discussion to have for some people because they don't like to talk about money or they feel they don't understand financial issues, but it is absolutely vital and critical to keeping a family functioning properly and keeping communication lines open. When people don't view money in the same manner and they spend money differently, it causes tension and financial difficulties, and if those are taken to an extreme before they are recognized, they can devastate a marriage.

In my particular case, it was a combination of decisions I made, and on top of that decisions my wife had made. Unfortunately we weren't talking about our finances, so when we finally realized the combined financial decisions we had made, it became very apparent that we had both misused credit. We had allowed credit to become too important in our lives, rather than focusing on the things that were really important to us. Pretty soon, our bills and debts owned us. Our passions were sapped out of us. It got to the point where we both had to worry about paying our bills, and those bills came with high interest rates so we never seemed to be paying down the principal we originally borrowed. We were constantly making payments to credit card companies and for loans, and we couldn't even tell you the products that were purchased because they were purchased a year or two earlier and now we were still paying off the balances with high interest rates month after month.

The Real Cost of Credit if Not Paid When Due

Let me give you an example, and I'm not using exact numbers here, but the story at least will make sense to people. If you borrow $5,000, and you just make the minimum payment that the credit card company tells you that you need to make each month, and if they are charging you 18 percent on the principal balance, it could take you more than twenty years to pay off the debt. In that time you would have paid more in interest than you actually borrowed from the credit card company. One of the issues you need to be aware of is that credit card companies have an interest in keeping you in debt, and so they offer you terms that make it look attractive. They will give you a minimum payment you need to make, rather than tell you how to pay off your balance. If you follow those minimum payment guidelines, you will always have a balance with the credit card companies, and you will be paying them for years, and decades – that is how they want it to be! A $5,000 bill could turn into a $12,000 payment plan…Ouch!

Credit Card Problems

Some of the problems that can occur are: you can start spending all the way up to your limit. That means if they make $500 available to you, you spend $500. So you've used up all of your credit, that means when your bill comes, you have all the regular bills you had prior to the credit, but in addition to that, now you owe $500 more. What happens is a lot of people forget what cash flow is. If you have the same amount of money coming in every month from your job, now, all of a sudden, you have to pay $500 out more in bills in order to pay off your credit card. Some people aren't able to do that. And what happens then is that you have a balance that carries forward and collects interest. Well, on every credit card bill there is something called a minimum payment, and a minimum payment is the lowest payment that the credit card company will accept. Oftentimes, it's less than 1-2 percent of the outstanding balance. So if you have a balance of $500-$600, they may say you have a minimum payment of $25. Well, if you make payments of $25 to pay off your balance, it would take you 5-8 years to pay off a $1000 balance. So one of the issues you need to be aware of is that minimum payment is something you should never, ever use. You should always pay off the balance in full, and if you can't pay the balance off in full then you shouldn't use credit, except for in emergencies.

You shouldn't tap out or use up all of the credit that is available to you, because credit can play a very important role if you ever run into an emergency. If your car breaks down, if you have a flat tire, if you need a tow, or any number of other emergencies occurs, you may need to have access to money immediately, and if you don't have cash with you or money in the bank, then having access to credit in order to get you through a difficult time will be very important. Therefore, it is important for you to establish credit and have credit available to you, but not to use it.

So, Why is Credit Important?

Well, if you had enough money to buy anything in the world whenever you wanted it, you'd never need credit. Unfortunately, there are very few people in the world who have such a strong financial position. Most people don't have all the money to buy whatever they want whenever they want it. A lot of people don't have enough money to buy what they need, let alone what they want.

So, some people want to make a purchase but they don't have the funds available at the time they want to buy something. It might be a real special sale. It might be an event to go to, like the Superbowl. It might be an emergency situation like a car breaking down, and so it's possible that you have money coming to you soon, but for a short period of time you need money to help pay the bills. If you own a small company, and you need to buy inventory, you're going to have expenses before you have revenue coming in from a customer. During that time period you might need somebody to offer you credit to pay your suppliers. If you have a reputation for being trusted and paying your bills on time, then you might be considered a good credit risk. But if you have a history of not paying your bills, of neglecting your responsibilities, or of making late payments, or defaulting on your debts, then you might be considered too risky ever to extend money to.

What Do Banks and Lenders Look for?

What the banks and lenders look for is your history—how you've handled your history with credit. That means it's important for you to establish a credit history in order for them to have information to draw from. I suggest you open a basic credit card with a limit of say $500, and show some history by making purchases on your credit card and paying off the balance. Now some people have said if you have a credit card and you always pay your balance off you will never establish a credit history because you never carried the balance forward. My personal viewpoint after everything I've been through is you should **do everything you can to be your own bank**. Don't rely on credit cards to issue you credit, and don't play games where you try to convince yourself you need to pay things off over time.

Look at Credit Card Issuers like Drug Pushers

I would look at credit card issuers at the same way I would look at somebody trying to sell drugs to you and get you hooked and addicted. Their role in life is to try to get you to use their credit card and to have a balance at all times. Your role is to protect your money and to protect your interest, and to build up savings so that you can become self-sufficient.

Credit Trouble? Where Does it Start?

How do people get into problems with credit? I say the first reason is **they don't understand what credit is**, and credit is basically eating into your future ability to use your own money by spending it today. Spending tomorrow's money today. **They don't manage their credit;** they don't understand that if a balance is not paid off in full, then it accumulates with a high interest rate. Also there are fees and expenses, there are late charges. Oftentimes if somebody looks at his credit card statements and what he's paid to the credit card companies, he'll find that if he borrowed $5,000, he may end up, in essence, between late fees and interest rates, with a 20-25 percent charge just to have access to that money. Also, some people just get into problems because **they're addicted to buying**. They're addicted to shopping, and they believe shopping makes them feel good, so they'll go out and shop. And if they don't have the money, they're not going to feel good, and they want to feel good so they go out and shop. But they don't shop with their money because they don't have any so they go out and use credit cards, and when they use credit cards to shop for those reasons, *they're going to get into a vicious cycle.*

FICO Scores

FICO scores are a standardized scoring system used to provide lenders a way to evaluate whether or not you would be a good or bad credit risk. It accumulates all the available credit in your name, and your payment history so that the reporting bureaus—Trans Union, Experian, and Equifax—store all of that information so every time you have a credit card or a loan, that becomes part of your credit history, which is stored in your credit bureau's credit systems. They use formulas (undisclosed to the public) to determine a score. If the lower-score people get credit offered to them, they are offered very expensive terms, maybe 20 percent interest or higher. They might have high fees on their credit cards, and so the lenders will look at them and say they are not responsible with their credit, so they are going to charge higher interest rates on whatever loans they make. Everybody who lends money for the most part reports into the credit bureaus.

If you have a credit card, they are reporting your payment history. If you are making payments on time, that is also recorded. So if you've had credit for five or ten years, and you have a score, then people will price the available loans to you based on your credit score. They may say credit scores within a certain range are charged 15 percent, and credit scores lower than that are charged 20 percent, and credit scores in the lowest range may not get credit loans offered to them. That's how the scoring system works: how they determine your score is based on a number of criteria, one of which is the amount of money made available to you as compared to the debt that you have.

For instance, if you have a credit card with a limit of $2,000, and you have $1,000 of balance on your credit card, 50 percent of your available credit is being used. That would be considered worse than somebody who has only a $100 balance on a card that offers $2,000. So if your balances are close to your limits on your credit cards, this will reflect poorly on your score. And that aspect of your score is about 33 percent of your total score.

FICO scores are very important. Employers look at your credit-worthiness, bankers and lenders look at your credit-worthiness, and business associates will look at how you've handled your credit. There is a lot of controversy about the use of scores, because the consumer does not have any say in terms of how it's calculated, and they don't have a lot of say in terms of what is reported to the three primary credit bureaus. It's important for every consumer to stay on top of what is happening to her credit, her history that is being reported to the credit bureaus, as well as her identity due to the high volume of identity theft. Monitoring your credit score is helpful to identify right away if you're a victim of identity theft, as well as to identify if somebody has stolen credit cards, misused your credit, or reported false information.

As a consumer, maintaining a good credit history is important, so that you can have access to credit in the future. Maintaining a good FICO score is based on making your payments on time, not having late payments, not defaulting on your payments, and not extending yourself up to or beyond the credit limit you've been given. So, one of the most important ways to keep a good score is to know how much credit has been extended to you and what your amount of debt is.

Don't Let Banks and Credit Card Companies Run Your Life...That is NOT living

These are the things that will happen if you allow credit cards to run your life. If you misuse credit, or abuse credit, or don't understand it and get yourself in trouble, credit card companies and banks calling will be a daily part of your life, perhaps even credit collection agencies. You will constantly be dealing with the hassle of trying to balance your bank accounts and your funds in order to pay bills. You will feel as if you are inferior and have a complex that makes you feel unable to handle your own affairs, which takes away your confidence and self-esteem. You will constantly be feeling stress, and you will have communications battles going on between you and anybody else in your family whenever somebody wants to spend money. Understand that you are under financial strain. It is a horrible situation to be in, yet, you can be cured and the situation fixed. The only way to fix it is to deal with it directly. *Hiding from it and denying that it is a problem only makes the problem worse, and could have an even more devastating impact.*

When a family is under stress and the wage earners are not managing their financial affairs responsibly, that can be seen by the children in the marriage. It can also be seen by everybody who is considered friends of the married couple because the added stress goes into every part of a marriage and every part of their lives. I've experienced this firsthand, and I can tell you that if it weren't for our ability to draw a line in the sand and say, "this is the end of the use of credit," I don't know how we would be living with each other because finances had brought such a devastating aspect to our relationship. **It also limits you from being able to make any plans about your future.**

You CAN Take Control

I'd like to end this section on a more positive note by saying you can take control. You can tell the credit card companies and the banks that you're going to pay back under your terms. They don't like to hear that, but that's too bad. While you don't want to destroy your credit or your score, **this is your life**. It is your money, and **you always have options** available to you up to and including wiping out the debt entirely. If you choose to wipe out the debt entirely, that will follow you for a period of up to ten years or longer on your public record. However, for some people, that might be necessary. All I can suggest is that you talk to a professional who is in the area of credit counseling to gain a better understanding of exactly what your issues are and how to handle them.

Is It Too Late?

What do you do if you've used credit cards and you find yourself in a situation where you feel that you've gone beyond your means and you can't pay off your debts and maintain positive cash flow?

Unfortunately, this is a problem all too common in our society. I believe the financial crisis has helped people recognize just how much credit a lot of families used. For those people who have overused credit cards and now find themselves with high, outstanding balances paying high interest rates, they feel as though they'll never be able to get out from underneath it. **I'd like to say <u>there is hope</u>, and it's not as devastating as you might think.** The first thing you need to do is to **be willing to cut your ties with credit cards and credit card companies.** It may seem hard; it may seem as if you're doing the impossible. It may also seem counterproductive because once you get rid of your cards you're going to be getting rid of the credit available to you, which could have a negative impact on your score. This is where you have to make some very well thought-out decisions. If you can take your credit cards, put them into a safe deposit box, hide them and never touch them, you will continue to have credit made available to you and you can pay off your balances.

What do you do if you have large credit card bills coming every month? First you need to understand that if you don't have any money in your savings and if you run into an emergency, you are going to have to come up funds somehow. This means you are creating your own problems by forcing yourself to dip into credit because you've never had any money in savings. It's absolutely critical that you have enough in savings, and most financial planners consider enough in savings to be three-six months' worth of your normal living expenses.

My final comment before I close out is simply this: my experience with credit card companies is that they have helped me during times when I've needed access to credit. They have also provided easy access to credit during the years when having easy access was fairly common, and then on a dime they turned and withdrew credit available, which had a damaging impact on me only because I hadn't paid off all my balances right away. So in the end I created my own problems by buying on credit and using that credit, rather than paying off my balances. At the end of the day, all blame will lie on the consumer, not on the credit-card issuer. That being said, if you find yourself having issues with credit card companies and you're trying to restore credit and you're trying to work to correct the situation, you have to do it with an empowering attitude. Be part of the process. Dictate some of the terms back to them just like they are dictating terms to you, and then come up with a mutually agreeable solution. Make your word your honor. **This will be the beginning of restoring your credit.** And it may be the beginning of restoring your relationships with people and values that really matter to you.

FINAL NOTE

BY JOHN GROLEAU

We all want our children to be more successful than we are. All parents want their child to have a better lifestyle and not make the same mistakes they did. That's normal. But the biggest mistake we can make is not really accepting our children for who they are and what their gifts are and instead trying to reincarnate them to be something else. This happened with my youngest son, Christopher. After one year of college, he has made the choice to go into the military and stop attending school for the time being. While it wasn't our first choice for Chris, I really believe that a tour in the military will provide the opportunity to develop the self-discipline and organizational skills that are lacking right now. Layla and I have been pleasantly surprised from the correspondence and phone calls we've gotten from Chris while in basic training. He's loving it! He even enjoyed the "Red Phase" (pain phase ☺) and has been a source of encouragement to his fellow trainees. Go figure. It was just what the doctor ordered. Accepting your children for who they are—not resigning yourself to it, and there is a difference—but accepting your student's gifts and where they are in life is the key to their life success.

I have a sign in my shower and another one taped to my computer monitor that I stole from Dr. Wayne Dyer, and it says, "I am whole and perfect as I was created." I think if we, as parents, would repeat that mantra to ourselves daily, especially when we are about to have a discussion with our children about schools, career choices, GPAs, and ACT scores, our family lives would be much more peaceful.

It's been a pleasure to help you navigate the strange and often challenging waters that accompany planning for your child's education. My family and I will continue to help you and your family as much as possible by providing you with the most current information possible for your planning. Please visit our website at http://www.lighthousecollegeplanning.com/

APPENDIX

8th GRADE AGENDA

1) Purpose of working together **(identify-plan-position yourself for college entrance)**

2) **Complete/Review** Student Information Sheet (note student responses for career clues)

3) **Discuss preparing for college admission:**

GENERAL COLLEGE ADMISSION REQUIREMENTS

The following are a list of general college admission requirements. During our time working with you, we will discuss each criterion with regard to your educational experience and personal goals. We will help you gain an understanding of how to improve your status in each category as you progress through your high school years.

1. CORE CURRICULUM 4-4*-3-3*-2/4*
   - Math—4 Years*
   - English—4 Years
   - Sciences (Lab Courses)—3 Years*

- Social Studies—3 Years
- Foreign Language—2 Years Required, 4 Years Recommended*
- *Varies Depending on Institution and/or Major
- (See reverse side of page for more details regarding curriculum recommendations)

2. Grade Point Average-GPA

3. Rank In Class- RIC

4. Percentile-%

5. ACT/SAT SCORES

6. EXTRACURRICULAR ACTIVITIES (including clubs, sports)

7. LEADERSHIP EXPERIENCES

8. VOLUNTEER EXPERIENCES

9. JOB SHADOWING/INTERNSHIPS IN YOUR FIELD OF INTEREST

10. PART TIME WORK EXPERIENCES

11. OTHER EXPERIENCES (summer camps, travel)

12. NON-SCHOOL RELATED INVOLVEMENT (community organizations, church)

Emphasize:

High School Coursework:	Stay in math, science, foreign language
High School Grades:	Get good grades-get help if needed Take any school testing seriously
High School Involvement:	Get involved in extracurriculars (sports and clubs) Take on leadership positions Do volunteer work

4) Introduce Career Cruising Website (almost high schools have Career Cruising or Naviance)

Step 2: Explore a Career Profile

There are hundreds of occupation profiles in Career Cruising and a number of ways to search for them, including keyword, search by index, and the Career Selector. For now, try the Search by School Subject.

- On the left side of the main page, click on EXPLORE CAREERS
- Click on SEARCH BY SCHOOL SUBJECT
- Select a subject
- Select an occupation

Browse through the occupation profile using the blue buttons on the left to find information about various aspects of the career, including job description, working conditions, earnings, and related resources. The Education section of each profile includes direct links to related college programs.

Each career profile also has a printer-friendly version, which you can access by clicking on the gray Printer-Friendly Report button at the bottom of the menu on the left.

Step 3: Multimedia Interviews

Each career profile contains two multimedia interviews with people in that occupation. Each person answers key questions about their experiences, what a typical day is like, what they like and don't like about their job, as well as advice for people interested in entering that career.

- Click on one of the names in the Photos & Interviews section on the left side of the occupation profile screen

Use the blue buttons on the left to navigate through the various sections of the interview. To play sound and video clips, click on one of the small icons next to the Likes, Dislikes and Advice buttons. The multimedia clips are available in Windows Media Player and in QuickTime. If your computer does not have either of these program installed, they can be downloaded for free.

- (Discuss Handout)

5) Introduce the "Who I Am" Essay

Welcome aboard! We are sincerely interested in helping you prepare for college and life! And there's a lot of work ahead for all of us to make sure this happens! We are prepared to monitor your high school academic planning, alert you to important test preparation and test dates, assist you with college and university selection, application and admission procedures, and assist you with finding and developing a career path which will be satisfying, and rewarding. We won't leave a stone unturned to provide you with everything you will need to be successful in college and life! Are you ready to get started? We are!

Believe it not, the next 3 to 4 years of your life are going to fly by. We haven't a minute to waste—and we've just met! We need to get to know you as quickly as possible. So, here's the first step your will take to ensure a great start toward your future.

In paper format, create a paragraph for each topic telling us all about you in relation to the following information. Don't leave out a thing! Don't write this all at once. Consider doing a couple of paragraphs each time you write.

Entitle your paper **(Your name)-WHO I AM**

Family dynamics (Share whatever you would like regarding your family. For example: Do you have siblings? Where do you fall in the birth order of children in the family? What is special about your family? What kinds of activities do you and your family enjoy doing together? Which parent do you tend to lean on the most? Why is that?)

School life (What is your attitude toward school? What is the best part of your school day and what about it is rewarding for you? What activities are you involved in and what makes them satisfying to you)

Personal life (What do you enjoy doing in your spare time and what makes the activity pleasurable for you? What are some things you absolutely dislike and what makes them unappealing to you? Have you experienced any barrier(s) that you have had to overcome and how did you get past these barriers? What did you learn from this experience (s)?)

Personal characteristics (What are some characteristics that make you the unique person that you are? What is your strongest strength? In what situations have you applied this strength? What was the reward? What is a weakness you have discovered in yourself? How has it given you trouble? What is an action you could take to compensate for this weakness?)

Career consideration (what are you thinking about as a career? What/who lead you in that direction? What makes you believe that this career area is suited to you?)

The WHAM factor (what are 3 things you would like us to know about you that you have not already commented on).

Freshman Year

1. Enjoy School! And not only as a prelude to college but as a place where you are developing as a student and as a person.

2. Develop a 4 year plan of coursework. Base your course selections on your ability and strive to be "challenged."

3. Establish strong study habits and time management techniques. Get help if you need it!

4. Develop a reading plan that includes newspapers, magazines, and books.

5. Work to enhance your reading and writing abilities and vocabulary proficiency.

6. Pursue extracurricular activities and perhaps investigate new activities in which you would like to participate.

7. **Keep track of volunteer hours on tracking sheet (We should include online access)

8. Keep your grades up. Good grades open many doors!

9. Think about your interests and how those interests might translate into career options. But keep your options open. Investigate lots of possibilities.

10. Meet with your school counselor. Find out where the information regarding career planning and college planning are located in your school. Which websites would your counselor recommend for career and college information?

10. Consider an interesting summer job, travel, or other learning experience.

11. Plan your sophomore year with care. Take classes appropriate for you. Push yourself but know your limits. Colleges look carefully at your classes—not just your grades. A strong college prep program is important!

Current Tasks
Log Onto Career Cruising and Complete Matchmaker and My Skills Assessments
Log Onto Career Cruising or O-Net (http://online.onetcenter.org) & Complete Three (3) Career/Occupational Searches
Log Onto Career Cruising School Selector & Complete Three (3) College Searches (Utilizing The College Research Questions)
Visit A Local College Campus and Complete Campus Visit Journal
Submit Final 9th Grade Transcript/Assessments
Submit 10th Grade Course Selections

Sophomore Checklist

❏ Meet with your high school counselor. Ask what you should do this year to prepare for college.

❏ Maintain strong study habits and time management techniques.

❏ Continue to pay attention to college information – website, books, magazines, etc. Learn where to find reliable information about college.

❏ Work to enhance your reading and writing abilities and vocabulary proficiency. Assess your strengths and weaknesses and work on weaknesses.

❏ Keep your grades up. Keep copies of your best writing.

❏ Target your major activities. Focus on participating in extra-curricular, leadership, and volunteer activities. Log these activities and post them on a resume. Also keep and post records of any performances/events/awards you receive.

❏ Think about those qualities which would make a college a "right fit and feel" for you. What size is best? Do you have location preferences? Visit some!

❏ Pay attention to what friends and others are saying about their college experiences.

❏ Sit in on a few meetings with college representatives who visit your school; attend a college night or college fair.

❏ Enroll for practice college entrance exams this year; the PSAT (to prepare for the SAT) or PLAN (to prepare for the ACT). Ask your counselor which is best for you.

❏ Think about your interests and how those interests might translate into career options. But keep your options open. Investigate lots of possibilities.

❏ Plan your junior year schedule carefully. Take classes appropriate for you: push yourself but know your limits. Colleges will look carefully at your class selections (not just your grades). A strong, college preparatory program balanced with courses in English, mathematics, social studies, science and languages is important.

❏ Consider an interesting summer job, travel, or other learning experience.

10th Grade Tasks/Assignments ** available online
Develop Resume/Portfolio
Attend College Fairs – **bring questions to ask college reps
Enroll/Take PLAN and/or PSAT Practice Tests
Complete Career/Occupations Searches
Complete College Searches ** fill out "What you want Checklist"
Visit Additional College Campuses and **Complete Campus Visit Journal For Each
Consider Career Vision for Aptitude Testing

10th Grade Tasks/Assignments ** available online
Submit Your Final 10th Grade Transcripts with Grades/Assessments
Submit Your 11th Grade Course Selections

Junior Checklist

❏ Be sure to review your Lighthouse Student Binder. You will be using these materials as you work through the college planning process.

❏ Meet and build a relationship with your high school counselor-make sure you are on track for high school graduation and college entrance requirements. Continue in 4 year course sequences.

❏ Continue to protect/raise your GPA—get assistance if necessary. Do you realize the payoff will be more colleges to choose from and a better chance for scholarship money?

❏ Continue to be involved in extracurricular, leadership and volunteer work. Colleges are not looking for a "jack of all trades" or a serial club joiner but they are looking for candidates who are well rounded—not just smart. Log all your activities onto your resume.

❏ Be cautious of all internet communications. Colleges are checking these closely.

❏ Check to make sure you have an appropriate email address for college communication. You can continue using your current email address for relatives and friends but develop one specifically to communicate with potential colleges. Make sure this email is very plain but professional.

❏ Make sure you have submitted all updated transcripts/assessments to Lighthouse for evaluation.

❑ Begin to develop a resume/portfolio. Update frequently. Portfolios may be required as part of the admission package if you are considering majoring in the arts (music, drama, fine arts). Find out what the requirements are for the portfolio or audition. There are colleges that offer scholarships for portfolios. Pay attention to the details and do not miss deadlines!

❑ Watch for information regarding PSAT/NMSQT exam. Online prep is available or you can request a copy of the Official Student Guide to the PSAT/NMSQT from your high school Guidance Office.

❑ Attend college fairs or college nights. Find out where some of these will be held and which colleges will be attending. This is a great place to either learn about a particular college or perhaps find information on a college you had not originally thought about.

❑ Find out when college representatives will be coming to your high school. Make it a point to meet a few of them. They are the true experts regarding the college they represent and would love to share some information with you.

❑ Be ready to seriously look at viable occupations and possible college majors. Use the Career Cruising or the ONET website: http://online.onetcenter.org for descriptions of occupations you have an interest in investigating. Use the Matchmaker/My Skills assessments or recommendations from your Career Vision consultation.

❑ Register online to take the December ACT (act.org) and request a score report. Online test prep is available. It may seem early to be taking this exam but it will give you a great idea of what improvements you may need to work on: time management, test strategies, anxiety issues, content. Do not report your score to any colleges as yet.

❑ Enroll in an ACT prep class to prepare you for the next round of ACT retakes (February, April, June). Use the results of your previous ACT exam/score report to help you focus on the areas you need to improve upon.

❑ Begin to think about what features you would like to have on a college campus. Use Career Cruising (school selector) to investigate what different colleges have to offer.

❑ Begin to develop a preliminary list of colleges you may want to visit. Look for colleges that have a strong program in your particular area of interest (major). Make sure you also have a "safety school" and a "back up plan" choice. As you visit colleges, be sure to journal your reactions.

❑ Start **seriously** visiting, comparing, compiling and understanding admission requirements for your preliminary college choices. Use the Academic Evaluation Questions and the CD in your student binder. Go over the Academic Evaluation Questions with your parents and highlight the questions that need to be answered in order for you to consider a particular college. As you compare colleges, email us your findings in groups of 3.

❑ Find out if you will you need SAT/SAT Subject tests as an admission requirement. If so, register to take these exams. Try to take these exams while subject matter is still fresh in your mind (spring). Ask your high school guidance counselor for the SAT Preparation Booklet.

❑ Register with NCAA if you plan on participating in D1 or D2 college sports. Keep in contact with your high school and/or club coach for recommendations on your ability level and possible colleges (ncaa.org). Need information regarding college athletics? Try ncsasports.com

❑ Be aware that if you attend a public Illinois high school, the Prairie State Achievement Exam is a graduation requirement. There is an

ACT component and it is FREE! Do a little review for this exam to increase your ACT score.

❏ Determine what experiences may help you decide upon a viable college major. We recommend that you do 2 job shadows or conduct 2 informational interviews in your area of interest. Also attempt to locate a part time job or develop an internship. These experiences will help you to more fully understand the entire realm of the occupation (major) in which you have an interest. Log these experiences onto your resume.

❏ Begin thinking about which instructors, coaches, etc. you will ask to write a letter of recommendation for you. Make sure you attach a "cheat sheet" to assist your instructors in understanding ALL your strengths inside and outside of the school setting. Make sure you thank those who are willing to write these letters for you.

❏ Register for any AP exams you would like to take and possibly use for college credit. Keep in mind that each college determines the criteria for accepting APs. You will need to find out from each college of interest what the criteria is in place.

❏ Look in your high school guidance office for the scholarships that were offered to this year's seniors. Make a note of those that you would like to apply for next year.

❏ Be thinking about topics for personal statements/essays for college admission. You will need to write, edit, revise and put together a final copy to attach to your college applications and/or use for scholarship opportunities and/or college campus interviews. The Lighthouse staff will gladly edit your rough draft. Make sure that after you have made your essay revisions that you email Lighthouse your final copy.

❏ Begin narrowing your list of potential colleges. Visit and revisit these colleges—spend the night, attend a class, talk to a professor in your interest area, speak with an upperclassman in your interest area. Get the "real deal!"

❏ Rank your college choices and email those to us.

❏ Discuss with your parents just how college will be financed. What will be YOUR financial responsibility toward college?

❏ Attend supplementary Lighthouse seminars (i.e. How to Get the Most Out of a College Visit).

❏ Begin filling out your college applications in August at start of senior year. Essays should be completed by September 1st. Pay close attention to deadlines. Make October 1st your "target date" to have all applications completed.

**Apply to Military Academies Junior year (if applicable)

11th Grade Tasks/Assignments
Check with School Counselor to ensure you are on track for High School Graduation and College Admission
Verify Appropriate Email Address for College Admission Correspondence
Submit Updated Transcripts/Assessments to Lighthouse (Grades 9-10)
Develop Resume/Portfolio Using Career Cruising and Update Frequently **Start with Resume template
Enroll/Take PSAT/NMSQT Test
Attend College Fairs
Develop a list of campus "must haves" to note when on a campus visit
Meet Three College Representatives When They Visit Your School
Complete Career/Occupational Searches, Utilize Matchmaker/My Skills/Career Vision/O-Net (http://online.onetcenter.org)

Register/Take December ACT (act.org), Request Score Report When Registering, Utilize Online Test Preparation
Log Onto Career Cruising School Selector & Complete Three (3) College Searches (Utilizing CD and Academic Evaluation Questions) Email Your Findings
Conduct at least three (3) College Visits. **Complete Journal for each
Enroll in ACT Preparation Course for February/April Test Dates
Log Onto Career Cruising School Selector & Complete Three (3) **College Searches (Utilizing The CD and Academic Evaluation Questions)—2nd Set Email Your Findings
Continue Campus Visits and Journal Your Reactions: during spring break-use **Campus Visit Checklist also
Register and Prepare for ACT retakes
Conduct two job shadowing/career informational interviews experiences for each career of interest
Request & Obtain Three (3) Letters of Recommendation **use checklist
Log Onto Career Cruising School Selector & Complete Three (3) College Searches (Utilizing The CD and Academic Evaluation Questions)—3rd Set Email Your Findings
Prioritize School Choices & Rank (#1-#9) and Email Results
Register/Take SAT Test (if required for college admission)
Enroll/Take Advanced Placement Tests (if applicable)
Write, Revise & Submit Personal Essay to Lighthouse ** see essay guidelines
Develop a full-fledged back-up plan and safety school
Begin College Applications (August)/Military Academies (July)
Compile List of Scholarships to research for Senior Year

Senior Checklist

FALL SEMESTER

❏ Review your Lighthouse Student Binder. The information contained within the binder will assist you in the college planning process

❏ Consider taking the Career Vision assessment very **seriously**. This is a tremendous help in assisting you with finding the most appropriate career path and college major

❏ Develop a plan as to how college will be paid for; what is **your** responsibility? Be aware of the term "total cost of attendance" vs "tuition." Don't forget to budget for application fees, standardized test score reports, transcript processing, transportation costs, etc.

❏ Recheck your email address for communication with college/ universities personnel

❏ Be mindful of ALL your internet communication; colleges are monitoring these

❏ Register for any ACT/SAT retakes. Make sure to do some "prep" work

❏ Register with NCAA if applicable-send in your best ACT score

❏ Develop or update your resume and continue to update on a regular basis

❏ Recheck your course selections against college admission requirements; **colleges are using the senior course schedule more heavily in the admission decision**

❏ Begin the scholarship search; check with your high school counselor as to how and where scholarship information is posted; open an account on collegeboard.com and look in your student binder for other helpful websites

❏ Request letters of recommendation from instructors:
  - Give instructors a "cheat sheet" to fully understand and highlight your strengths in and out of the classroom

  - Highlight what you would like emphasized in the letter

  - Request 2 to 3 signed copies of each

  - Send a follow up thank you letter or a box of chocolates

❏ Develop a strong personal statement/essay for application, scholarship and campus interview purposes; pay attention to instructions. Emphasize your personal beliefs and character

❏ Begin to thoroughly research the colleges of interest. Use the Academic Evaluation Questions and the CD for ease of comparison. Submit your research in groups of 3

❏ Narrow your college choices to 5 or 6; now rank these colleges in order of interest; make sure you have a "safety school" and a "back up" plan

❏ Continue to visit and **revisit** your priority colleges: **GET THE REAL DEAL AND BECOME THE EXPERT ON THESE COLLEGES (use the campus checklist and journal handout)**
  - Arrange for an overnight visit

  - Meet a professor of the department in which you have an interest

  - Talk to an upperclassman in your area of interest

  - Request a campus interview if you believe your high school record does not truly reflect your ability and talent

  - Obtain business cards or email address for later contact

  REMEMBER; "FIT"— "FEEL"—"AFFORDABILITY"

❏ Begin the college application process: do "rolling admissions" first

- Make sure you understand the pros and cons of applying with the common application (www.commonapp.org)
- Avoid common mistakes of redundancy and not following directions
- Make sure you are aware of application deadlines
- Make sure you are aware of ALL the documentation required (personal essay or statement, portfolio)
- Determine which ACT/SAT score(s) you are going to submit to colleges and request them from appropriate testing agency

❏ Complete your college applications-aim for being done by the first week of October; interested in ROTC? Check the deadline

❏ Continue to attend college fairs and/or meet college reps that come to your high school; these are valuable resources for updates on the colleges in which you have an interest. Most colleges appreciate your knowledge of the academic and social culture on campus

❏ Inquire as to when and where your high school will be hosting a Financial Aid Night and attend with a parent

❏ Request Mid-Year Transcripts to be sent to colleges you are still considering

❏ Conduct job shadowing to verify that the college major you are considering is appropriate for your career of interest

❏ Begin gathering information for the FAFSA (and CSS if applicable) financial aid forms

❏ Attend supplementary Lighthouse workshops

❏ Respond to all Lighthouse emails—this helps YOU keep on track in the college planning process

CLEARLY UNDERSTAND THAT COLLEGE ADMISSIONS ARE CONDITIONAL: IF YOUR GRADES FALL OR OTHER CIRCUMSTANCES ARISE, COLLEGES ARE FREE TO REJECT YOUR APPLICATION. **THIS IS NOT THE TIME FOR SENIORITIS!

Tasks
Discuss the realistic cost of attendance of colleges you are interested in-how will this be paid? Who is paying for what? What is YOUR responsibility?
Recheck your email address for college communication appropriateness
Be mindful of ALL your internet communications (colleges are monitoring)
Register with the NCAA Clearinghouse (if applicable)
Update your resume-continue to update regularly
Recheck your senior course selections (check against the admission requirements of your priority colleges)
Start investigation scholarship opportunities-start with your HS guidance department and look at collegeboard.com. Other sites are in your binder
Obtain the last of your letters of recommendation (if applicable)
Develop a strong personal statement/essay for college admissions and scholarships
Complete College Research; Submit Research in Groups of Three
Begin college applications and send in ACT scores directly from the testing company-do rolling admissions first
Attend college fairs/nights—touch base with reps from your priority colleges. Find out what is new on campus.

Visit and revisit your priority colleges as often as possible. Stay overnight, attend a class, meet a professor in your interest area, talk with an upperclassman in your interest area (questions are in your binder). Use the Campus Tour Checklist as a guide
Contact the colleges of interest-check to see if they have received all the documentation needed for admission consideration
Contact the financial aid office of the colleges of interest-check to see if any additional financial aid forms are necessary or supplementary to the FAFSA
Attend Financial Aid Night
Set up campus/scholarship interviews
Develop a back-up plan
Let your high school guidance department know if you will need to send out midyear transcripts-college admission is "conditional"
Start gathering information you will need for the FAFSA; file FAFSA Jan 1 and/or CSS
Do some job shadowing-make sure the occupation you are interested in is truly the major that you are considering for college admission
Check ROTC Deadlines (if applicable)
Attend ALL Lighthouse supplementary workshops

Senior Checklist

SPRING SEMESTER

❑ Contact the admissions 's office and the financial aid office at the colleges(s) you are considering; check to see if there are any other forms necessary to complete for the admission or financial aid process? Have they received all the necessary documentation to proceed with an admission's decision?

❑ Continue job shadowing or informational interviewing in occupations of interest. This is a great way to ensure you are on target with your college major. Do 2 per occupation so you can compare and contrast settings, demands, etc.

❑ Register for AP exams which will be taken in May; homeschooled students need to contact AP Services by March 1 to register for the May AP exams. Contact your local high school for additional information

❑ Keep revisiting your priority colleges-attend an event

❑ Send any award/scholarship letters that you receive to Lighthouse. Don't forget to send a thank you note to those groups or organizations that awarded you scholarship money!

❑ Recheck your college financing plan-are your arrangements to finance college in order? FAFSA filed? CSS profile required?

❑ Attend the Lighthouse Award Presentation for clarification and appeal process procedure

❑ Compare/accept a college financial aid package and mail in your deposit

❑ Send in a check for your college housing when you are accepted into any college you are seriously considering

❑ Withdraw your application from colleges that you no longer have any interest in attending

- ❏ Send in your final transcript to the college of choice. NCAA (if applicable) will require a final transcript as well
- ❏ Get updated on any immunizations and get a copy of your immunization record for those colleges that request this
- ❏ Attempt to work part-time and/or develop an internship in your area of interest. Concentrate on activities that will give you more insight into your career/college major
- ❏ Respond to all Lighthouse emails
- ❏ Attend Lighthouse supplementary workshops
- ❏ Enroll in the earliest Freshman Orientation program offered at the college of your choice so the classes/days/times/best professors will be available

Tasks
Find out the registration dates for SATs/SAT Subject Tests (if needed)
Set up campus/scholarship interviews
Sign up for May AP Exams (if applicable)
Keep revisiting priority schools-attend an event on campus
Continue your scholarship search-look for community sponsored scholarships-keep a folder of awards: scholarship name, amount received, renewable, renewable with restrictions
Send any award or scholarship letters to Lighthouse
Compare your award letters/packages
Attend the Lighthouse Award Presentation for clarification and appeal process requirements
Accept a college financial aid package and mail in a deposit
Continue to job shadow to ensure you have chosen a viable college major

Send immunization records with updates to the colleges that require this documentation
Notify the colleges that you are no longer considering
Take AP exams (if applicable)
Notify your High School Guidance Department where you need a final transcipt(s) sent to college and/or NCAA
Look for a summer job or develop an internship in your area of interest
Enroll in the eariiest freshman orientation program offered at the college of your choice

BEST WISHES AS YOU MOVE ON TO COLLEGE ENTRANCE!

Perspectives from Parents and Students:

THE GROLEAU FAMILY STORY

JOHN - FATHER OF FOUR AND FINANCIAL PLANNER

As a parent, having four kids in school and at one point three in college at the same time for two years makes me be able to say along with Bill Clinton, "I feel your pain." I know what it's like to go through this. I know the concern, the anxiety, the worry — academically, environmentally, and financially— about how you are going to get through this. And my families know that for anything I recommend, I have the experience to back it up.

In terms of students, I know what it's like not to know what you want to do with your life. I know what it's like personally to have no sense of direction through the educational process. I know what it's like to feel confused. I know what it's like to struggle with your relationship with parents getting through this. I think that having changed my major a bunch of times, not knowing how to pick a school, and also dealing with my own children has provided valuable life lessons. I believe that supporting the kids, rather than enabling them, helps them make great decisions of their own and is valuable to families and students alike.

How did the rest of the family influence me as a college financial planner?

With regard to my wife, it was a case of the cobbler's kids have no shoes. Even though I had been doing financial and educational planning for years my wife kept hounding me about when we were going to deal with the kids' college planning. And I kept putting it off, and putting it off, and putting it off. I guess one of the good things is that Layla, with enough gentle pressure, forced me to get on the stick and get moving on with Stephanie. I guess it goes back to the old expression, "Behind every successful man is a surprised mother-in-law."

So as a result of Layla's encouragement, I actually have three piggy banks on top of my credenza in my office. The biggest one says 'college,' the medium-sized one says 'wedding,' and the little itty bitty one says 'retirement.' And the reason is that's how most people plan their lives. They focus on college first, wedding second, and retirement last, when it should be just the opposite.

Layla, like many spouses, has really forced me to be a better manager of our own funds and also to have better direction and planning. Her encouragement got me in gear, and I developed a plan for all four kids which worked out well. I'm proud to say that at this point all four kids are going to be graduated from college and Layla and I will have no debt. That is something for which I am feeling not only very grateful and blessed, but proud of how we developed a good plan and put it into practice.

How did Stephanie influence me as a college financial planner?

All four of our kids are very different from one another. They are wonderful children, very bright, very capable; as I said earlier thank God they take after my wife. Stephanie has my best and worst qualities. She is a driven child, highly motivated, highly talented, and has little patience for fools. So as a college planner, I had some concerns when she looked at colleges. She wanted to be a marine biologist because that's what one of my majors was and we used to take the kids back to Maine every summer to visit family. We had a place right on the ocean where I grew up, and Stephanie loved the ocean. I remember when I was studying marine biology the starting salary wasn't very high, so I was also concerned about getting a job as a marine biologist because I knew there were people with PhDs who were swabbing the decks at Woods Hole Oceanographic Institute in Massachusetts.

So Stephanie really cemented in my mind the importance of Career Vision. Once we went through it, the Career Vision counselor told her marine biology would be bad for two reasons.

One, personality-wise she would die in a laboratory because she needs to be doing something different every day, and number two because her math scores are so high she would be bored if she didn't use math in her career. My wife said, "What about engineering?" and Stephanie said "I want to do something near the ocean," so the career counselor said "What about ocean engineering?" I never even thought about that before.

As a first child, Stephanie was really motivated and very responsible and responsive to suggestions. She really did an awesome job getting a job on campus with a professor, and as a matter of fact it only cost us about $7,000 a year to send her to a $37,000-a-year school. As a result, she was able to get her master's degree in engineering in 5 years, which is a major accomplishment The total cost for the master's degree was only about $5,000. Stephanie has always done a great job as a planner. But also realizing that being sensitive to her going to school in Florida, even though its only 3 hours away by plane, is still a long way away when you're 18. It's helped me have a little more perspective in terms of children's personalities and what they are capable of doing. For her, going far away from home was a good fit.

Shireen, who is my next child and a year younger than Stephanie, is a little different. Shireen was really unsure of her major. Growing up, she has always had a little bit of self doubt. As a matter of fact, even though she won a national writing contest in high school, when my wife and I suggested she join the school newspaper, her comment was, "I'm not good enough." At Career Vision, the counselor said, "You know, Shireen, you really need to have creative writing as part of your career or as an avocation, and by the way have you ever thought of being in the school newspaper? You would be really good at it." Shireen said, "Oh, that sounds like a good idea." Shireen helped me realize that sometimes as parents we have a big L on our foreheads for Loser, and really helped me to appreciate that utilizing third-party objective people to get the point across in a way that Mom and Dad cannot is sometimes essential. Because I do realize, and parents you should realize, that at some point for many of us, when we have teenagers our IQs will start going south of 100 the closer our children get to graduation. And at some point when they hit about 23 to 25 years old, miraculously, our IQs as parents will start to go up again. Shireen really wanted to be in a city. As much as Stephanie wanted to be near the ocean and near a beach, Shireen really wanted to be in a city and Chicago had to be the city, and she still wanted to be close to home. As a matter of fact, that first semester freshman year she was probably home every other weekend. And then second semester in January was kind of like "Uh, Shireen, are you still alive out there?" She just needed some time to get little bit of confidence and perspective and she was fine.

Now Michael on the other hand, our karma kid, normally pretty easygoing, took a more bullish stance and pushed back saying "You know what, I'll pay for this myself, I'm going to do it my way, and I'm going to go to school where I want to go to school." I looked at Michael and said, "Well, if that's the way you want to go, here's what you need to do." I gave him the names of a couple bankers and said "Why don't you go call these people up and see how much money they will lend you as a student." He came back from talking to one and I said, "So…what did they say?" and he said, "You know what they said!." I said, "let me guess," and made a 0 out of my fingers and said "Is this the number they gave you?" As a result Michael became a little more open to finding a different way. I was trying to work on compromising, but I also needed to find a place where Michael was going to be nurtured, and given lots of opportunities to be a big fish in the pond. He went go to a medium-sized school, The University of Dayton, where he found a very fruitful and nurturing environment. It was a perfect fit for him, he's made some great friends, done well in school, and he's made the best of his opportunities there.

Christopher has influenced me in different ways. Part of the concern I had for Chris was dealing with his issues. Christopher was diagnosed with ADD early on in elementary school, about 6th grade, and we also found out that he had an auditory processing problem which makes things like organizational skills and self discipline a huge struggle for him. So some of the things that we had to give thought to for Christopher was not only thriving in school but on a more basic level surviving in school. One of the options we had to think about was would he be better off going to a junior college for a year or two and then transferring? The advantage was that we would be able to keep an eye on him, and the disadvantage was we would be keeping an eye on him. I felt that he needed to kind of get away from Mom and Dad because it's easy for him to blame us and say, "You know, if it weren't for you and if I were living on my own, I would be doing OK and getting C's in my classes." Option two for Chris, and an option other parents can consider, especially in a program such as engineering, is to do what's called a 3+2. The student can go to a liberal arts school for three years where the professors are really going to mentor the child and pull the best out of them. The class sizes are small enough so they can develop a really close relationship with their professors, and then the last two years they can go to an engineering school like Illinois, Michigan, Dayton, Marquette, wherever it is. We had to wrestle with those options, and we finally decided to have him to go University of Dayton so that he could be with his brother for support. It was nice to have two kids in the same zip code for a change. Since Christopher is probably the quietest and most introspective of the kids, Michael's friends, who also had younger siblings in college, would probably pave the way for an easier transition from high school to college.

1949 – WE'VE COME A LONG WAY, BABY!

MEMERE GROLEAU

Following is a question and answer session I had with my mother about her experience with college. Enjoy!

QUESTION: What were the expectations of you going to college?

ANSWER: I was rather indignant but they wouldn't support my decision, and my brother Jerry was Mama's pet so anything Jerry wanted to do was fine and perfect.

QUESTION: Did the decision not to support you come from your being a woman and his being a man?

ANSWER: No, it was partly because he was mama's weakness. He was her pet. He just liked her. But he wasn't interested in going to school; he wanted to be a printer at the newspaper. So it's interesting because I could have gone as far as I wanted to actually, because the director at the school of nursing wanted me to go get my degree. My mother wasn't going to waste money on her daughter who wanted to go to school. In those days, I mean, a daughter going to school wasn't that important. However, in our community, the telephone office always paid nice wages, so if you really wanted to make a good living you could always become a telephone operator, but that wasn't my dream. So I told her I didn't care if she was going to help me pay for my schooling, I'd go out and work for a year and earn all the money I needed for my tuition. Then I'd go to college, and do what I wanted to do. So she said, "Well, in that case, if you're going to be so stubborn, I would help you pay for your college education."

QUESTION: Didn't you receive a job offer at the same time your mom agreed to help pay for your college?

ANSWER: Yes, I had applied to take the exams to become a telephone operator, and the day I was accepted at the school I had an appointment with the director, although I wasn't quite the age. I think I was supposed to be 20 and I wasn't quite 20. She said she would take me in just the same. When I got home I had a call from the telephone office saying I had a job if I wanted it, but that's not really what I wanted. I wanted to go into the school of nursing, so that's where I went.

QUESTION: When you were in high school, were there guidance counselors to help students decide what they wanted to do or where to go to college?

ANSWER: No, I think I had a classmate in high school who was interested in going into nursing and she had talked about it and that spiked my interest. However, she never did go into nursing, but I did and I enjoyed it and made a career out of it.

QUESTION: Was there any career guidance or skills evaluation?

ANSWER: No, no, nothing. If you had an inclination or your classmates happened to be taking about something, that's how you developed an interest. And there was nothing available to encourage you in any way, especially if your parents weren't encouraging you. My mother kind of ruled the roost. But if I'd wanted to, and she said she didn't want to, I would have gone to my father and he would have said yes and supported me. I could always get from my father whatever I wanted.

QUESTION: How much did it cost to attend St. Mary's School of Nursing?

ANSWER: It wasn't much, probably $300-$400 dollars, I don't recall if that covered the year or the whole 3 years or what. But, they gave us a stipend. So with the stipend I could make it through the three years. If I could make it through the first year and support myself, then with the stipend I could support myself through the other two years and complete.

QUESTION: Where did you live when you went to school?

ANSWER: At the school, in a dorm.

QUESTION: What did the school pay for?

ANSWER: Everything. But we used to work too. We'd help take care of patients that we had, and we worked different shifts: evening shifts, night shifts, and what have you. So we kind of really supported our education in that way.

QUESTION: Did they have a four-year Bachelor's of Nursing degree back then?

ANSWER: I think they did in college but they were very expensive; you know, you really had to have bucks if you wanted to go to college in those days, it was quite prohibitive, actually.

QUESTION: You graduated in 1949; what did you do after that?

ANSWER: I did night duty for a couple of years. I got kind of tired because I didn't get too much sleep during the day, went out to the beaches and went swimming or skiing. And so after a couple of years of that I decided I wanted more, so I went to go see the director of nurses and she offered me this job of being student health nurse, and help with the three college professors who used to come and teach at the school, chemistry, anatomy and physiology, and microbiology; they were from Bates college. I used to set up the science labs for them, and take care of the labs after they were done with the students. That was kind of neat; I liked that. And then the nun who was the director of nursing offered me these scholarships — she wanted me to go on anyhow, so she found these scholarships for me.

QUESTION: Why did she want you to go to college?

ANSWER: To get my degree so I could come back and teach at the school, and she probably saw potential in me that I didn't, but anyhow she wanted me to go out and get my degrees so I could come back and teach at the school. So that summer in the early 50's (I had only been a nurse for a few years), I went to Catholic University in Washington, D.C., and I had a cousin who was in the service. He was married, and they lived just across the river from where the university was, so I got to see them fairly often. They'd pick me up on weekends and I'd go have dinner there, or they'd take me out for a ride around.

QUESTION: When did you start teaching advanced classes?

ANSWER: Well, mostly I was an assistant to three college professors. About that time I was only teaching basics in nursing. The students, you know, like how to give baths and make beds, stuff like that. Just the real basics. I was a good nurse, and I guess the director probably liked me too. I was kind of likeable in those days.

QUESTION: So you kept taking more classes toward your degree?

ANSWER: Yes, I did that through Boston University, they had an extension program with the University of Southern Maine in Portland, and I took courses there, I'd commute there, day courses. And that was interesting. And they'd present your courses so they had courses later in the day so you could work your day and then a group of us would get in the automobiles and go down and take the courses.

QUESTION: This was still before you got married?

ANSWER: Yes, this was before I got married. Oh, and that's when the hospital opened a critical care unit, and the director wanted to put students there. And she wanted me to handle that and I said, "No way!" but she said, "I want you there, I know I can depend on you," and I said "No way, my father and all of his siblings, by the time there were in their 50's they had coronaries or had died of strokes, and I want to have nothing to do with it," but she said, "The more you know about it, the more you will feel comfortable about it". That was probably around the mid 50's; I still wasn't married.

QUESTION: When did you go back to complete your bachelor's degree?

ANSWER: I started taking summer sessions at St. Joseph's college in North Windham in the early 70's. I always enjoyed learning, and your father would just encourage it and what I wanted to do was fine with him (Joseph Groleau). And we'd leave mid-afternoon, director was very liberal and would allow this, so I could take off with the other girls and we'd head to Portland, attend the classes, and come back.

QUESTION: Who paid for your bachelor's degree?

ANSWER: I think I paid for all of them.

QUESTION: Did the hospital pay for any of it?

ANSWER: Yes, they picked up so much of the courses that I took, so I figured it's just like giving myself a raise. They wouldn't give me the money anyhow in a raise, so if I took the courses; sometimes they paid for all the courses. Most of the time they paid for a good part of the courses, so it's just like giving myself a raise, and at the same time I was just insuring my future. Worked out good.

QUESTION: Where did you get your master's?

ANSWER: University of Southern Maine, Portland.

QUESTION: What was your GPA?

ANSWER: I actually got a 4.0 for my bachelor and master's degrees.

QUESTION: What were your degrees in again?

ANSWER: My bachelor's was in psychology. You used to tell me to stop trying to psych you out — that was a lot of fun. "Stop trying to psych me out again!" But my master's was in education. My bachelor's was in psychology.

QUESTION: Looking back, from 1949-1987, is there anything you would have done differently?

ANSWER: I think if my mother had not discouraged me, I would have accepted those Rockefeller foundation scholarships from the Rockefellers in New York. I think that would have had a lot of future in it. They (the scholarships) just paid for your education in anything I wanted, I think.

QUESTION: How did you find those scholarships?

ANSWER: I had to apply for them. The director of the school wanted me to apply for them, the nursing school. And that would have been no problem, I would have been accepted anyhow, but my mother just put the kibosh on that.

QUESTION: What was it about the scholarships she didn't like? How much were they for?

ANSWER: I was going to be away from home, what's the matter with you? I was a little green girl, I would have had to go study in New York, I don't recall where, and I have no idea. Wherever the Rockefellers were supporting the scholarship, I guess. They paid for everything, all paid for. Isn't that stupid, not to accept them? My mother wouldn't hear it. Her little girl went into New York all by herself, her little green girl from Maine.

QUESTION: Is there anything else you'd like to share?

ANSWER: I had a good nursing career. I could have gone wherever I wanted to go in that career, no problems whatsoever and no cost to me. Just my supposed "smarts."

QUESTION: Do you have any advice for someone who wants to go into the nursing field?

ANSWER: I don't know if I would encourage anyone to go into the nursing field. I think the nursing field was safe then. But today, with all the serious diseases and illnesses that are out there, I don't think it's that safe of a profession to get into, really. And I don't know if it is as respected and looked up to as it used to be.

The Groleau Family

"MIXED NUTS!"

BY MICHAEL GROLEAU

As a prelude, I am just stating that the Groleau Family is extremely creepy and hard to understand, and even with an easy-to-read manual such as this it can be quite a challenge to understand the true sarcasm and absolute ridiculousness of the individuals and the family as a whole.

First, if you are to understand the unnatural offspring, you must comprehend the parents of these beasts. The most primary parent, as the male and natural leader of the family, is John Steven Groleau. Bearing a strange resemblance to his son Michael Groleau, John is extraordinarily handsome and devious. You can recognize him by his strange lack of hair or his sharp wit, which has only been honed by its use on his spawn. Master of tools, Mr. Groleau has a strange affinity for wood. Maybe it is the fact that wood can be used to spank his children or that it has other uses, but John is quite the woodworker.

Besides woodworking, John enjoys telling high schoolers which school they can go to so as to inconvenience them fully and make their parents happy. He is a teenager's nightmare. A mix of sarcasm and bullying that comes together in a bout of wrestling, at which only the most handsome and strongest of men can beat him. This is John Groleau. Fear him, feed him, but for God's sake don't race him, because as he is falling behind, he will shoot you in the behind. How pleasant.

Strength – Cooking skills
Weakness – New shiny tools

Following after her sneaky husband comes the ever-watchful mother. Mrs. Layla Marie Groleau. Oh, the witch. She frequently covers up her secret identity by dressing up as a witch on Halloween. Oh, that treacherous woman. Tricking her students and other children into liking her, only to steal their lunch chocolate from them when they are least suspecting. And contrary to belief, she will not melt, proved to be true by her frequent crying episodes. It is still a medical mystery as to why and how she can cry so much and not wither for lack of water, but the overflowing sewer pipes behind the Groleau abode will testify to her many tears. Whether because of actual sadness, overflowing joy, a successful thievery of another child's lunch, or just having not cried in the last couple of hours, the tears will keep coming, so beware being drowned in the sudden flash floods. Besides being a master trickster, Mrs. Groleau has a famous stubborn streak which can only be outlasted by the illustrious Stephanie Groleau, or by a long phone call from the beautiful Shireen Groleau. The sons are left to rot in the dirt as they argue futilely with the overwhelming power of motherhood.

Strength – Wonder Woman is always strong
Weakness – Chocolate - dark

The oldest and most wise of the children, especially in matters of the parents, is Miss Stephanie Groleau. Known as Befie by the most handsome sibling, Michael Groleau, Stephanie has a streak of determination so great it could blot out the sun. As an ocean engineer, the oldest sibling gets a view much better than that of the rest of her unfortunate family left behind in Ohio and Illinois, which are abundant in cornfields and little else. Besides being determined, Befie seems to have stolen the stubbornness from the almighty mother and nurtured it so that it sprouted as Chris did from the midget he used to be. Anyway, she seems to be the only one who can out-stubborn Wonder Woman. Even though she is stubborn, she is tricksy too. She uses the womanly fault of having a lack of muscle to rope her strong brothers into doing chores involving lifting, or really any chores that she deems unfit for someone who should be able to move objects with her mind, so great is her wisdom.

Strength – strong-willed

Weakness – nice cute boys

Trotting behind Stephanie, in her new knee-high boots, comes the second evil sister, Shireen Elizabeth Groleau. Master of fashion and of boys, Shireen is a dominant woman. Showing the same weakness as the mother, Shireen tends to leak at the most untimely moments and for the most unlikely of reasons. Starting at a young age, Shireen took it to be her duty to deprive her brothers of all possessions of which she deemed them not worthy or which could be put to better use under her watchful eye. Winning was also a big priority; rules, not so much. So using her sharp wits and gullible brothers, she is able to trick people into thinking she is much smarter than is actually true. As she grew into the gorgeous fashion queen that she is today, Shireen learned how to play follow the leader, with her as the leader, and showed Chicago that she is the Queen and they need to understand that and follow her. Somehow she has been able to pass off her strange resemblance to a bean as being queenly, and Chicago follows quietly at her high heel.

Strengths – Fashion sense

Weakness – New expensive outfit

Next in line is the elusive Pimpernel. Not only is he extremely handsome, he is intelligent and an Eagle Scout. Stand in line, please, for any job offers. This devilish rogue has spent many hours pretending to plan for inconceivable pranks only to have them fall apart and resort to rolling people up in rugs like a large cigar. Mr. Michael Joseph Groleau resembles his father in many respects, yet as surely as the father's looks are failing, Mike's are only increasing. This young college student puts a lot of faith in God and incorporates his faith in his everyday life. Not only does he have a strong faith, but he has a rock to build on; as long as the rocks aren't used to throw at deserving miscreants. Mike is built on sarcasm and a strange sense of humor. It gets him through the day, and it makes him able to comfort other people and help them feel more comfortable. It also makes it easier for him to make fun of people without their understanding him, leaving him guilt-free. In addition, Mike tends to have an extraordinary amount of energy and uses it erratically throughout the day. It has given him the uncommon ability to fall asleep wherever and whenever he feels the need. Quite an accomplishment, I must say. Also, Mike has a love for movies that is unmatched by all but the most socially shy. A certain quality taken from his mother seems to be the unnatural love for chocolate chips. Dark or semi-sweet, they hold a certain irresistible power over the young college student.

Strength – Radiant Joy, Unrestrained craziness
Weakness – Well-planned pranks

Last but not least is the beast. Chris has outgrown even his muscular brother and continues to fuel his growth with Kung Fu: basically a method of revenge for all the times Mike exerted his overwhelming muscles on the weaker Chris. Even though Chris can sleep for almost the entire day, he still seems to be able to lie on his bed for the rest of the day. Having the amazing chance to spend the most time with his parents as he is the only one left in the household, Chris seems to have gained the ability to annoy them fully at any time he wants — comes in helpful when he doesn't want to do chores or something. Even so, Chris seems to be the calmest of all the siblings. Most of us have something that makes us just insane, and Chris is somehow able to keep calm through it all. What the heck.

Strength – Calmness

Weakness – Sleeping in too long

So I hope that this manual is both instructive and entertaining because it took long enough to type, and if you didn't enjoy it the first time then make sure to read it again because I spent the time to write, so you should spend at least as much time enjoying it.

Clearly, the most important persona in the manual is the Pimpernel but if you feel a connection to the others, feel free to think on their complexities too.